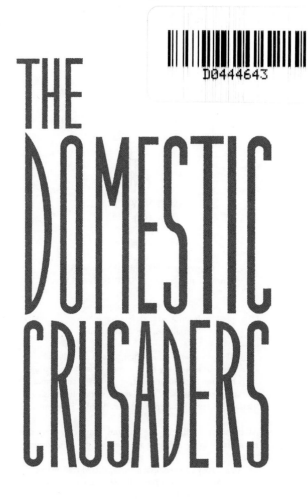

THE DOMESTIC CRUSADERS

D0444643

McSWEENEY'S BOOKS

SAN FRANCISCO

www.mcsweeneys.net

Copyright © 2004, 2010 Wajahat Ali
Introduction copyright © 2010 Ishmael Reed

Cover artwork by Daniel Krall
Interior artwork by Connie Sun
Special thanks to Shazia Kamal

McSweeney's and colophon are registered trademarks
of McSweeney's, a privately held company with
wildly fluctuating resources.

ISBN-13: 978-1-936365-17-3

THE
DOMESTIC
CRUSADERS

A TWO-ACT PLAY *by*

WAJAHAT ALI

introduction by

ISHMAEL REED

INTRODUCTION

by ISHMAEL REED

Appearing before the National Council of Teachers of English, I read a poem by a canonized poet and one by a student and asked the audience to identify which was which. Fifty percent said that the student was the canonized poet and fifty percent said that the canonized poet was the student. If I had read from Wajahat Ali's work, I'd guess that seventy-five percent would identify Ali as the canonized author.

In 2001, Wajahat came to my classroom equipped with the kinds of tools that might eventually lead to his becoming a great writer. He possessed a knowledge of language that he seemed able to draw upon effortlessly; he had a rich imagination; and most of all he had a good ear, and the ability to draw characters who were distinct from one another. Wajahat also appreciated history and culture. He was the only one in my class to correctly identify the editor of T. S. Eliot's "The Waste Land"—Ezra Pound. He was the only one who could answer my questions about the Crusades or the Mughal Dynasty. Oftentimes we discussed international cinema and obscure foreign movies.

My first impression of Wajahat reminded me of my first impression of Frank Chin. In the early 1970s, I sent Frank's play *The Year of the Dragon* to the producer Chiz Schultz, whom I'd met in New York. He got it staged at the American Place Theatre in 1974, and eventually it aired on PBS. Some credit this play with having launched an Asian American artistic renaissance. Would a play by Wajahat Ali have the same effect for Muslims and Pakistani Americans?

After 9/11, Wajahat stopped coming to class for about three weeks; he was overwhelmed with his leadership activities in the UC Berkeley Muslim Student Association. When he returned, he read aloud a four-page story, "Bulbus and Rotunda's Fiftieth Wedding Anniversary," about a couple of feuding, married ogres who secretly plot to kill one another. After hearing the story, I told him to see me after class.

Years later, Wajahat told me he was afraid I would chew him out for missing three weeks of classes. Instead, I told him he was a natural playwright—dialogue and characters were his strengths. I told him that instead of turning in short stories, he should write a play about an ordinary Muslim Pakistani American family. One that would counter the ugly stereotypes promoted by a media that sees its profits in raising fear and dividing ethnic groups and races.

I recalled my colleague Lawrence DiStasi's comment after viewing Frank Chin's stereotypes-shattering play—he said that the Chinese American family Frank presented could have been Italian American. (For better or worse, we all have families.) Wajahat's characters can be found in every kitchen drama—the sort of play that concerns itself with food, dating, sibling rivalry, intergenerational conflict, humor, and pathos.

I suggested that Wajahat read family plays by Eugene O'Neill, Arthur Miller, and Lorraine Hansberry. I said he'd have to submit twenty pages in order to pass the course. He said that he had no experience in playwriting, but he turned in his twenty pages. Over the next two years, I kept emailing him, and encouraged him to finish his play—which he did, five to ten pages at a time. In 2003, he gave me his first completed draft. Not long after that, I turned him over to my partner since 1965, Carla Blank, who became the dramaturge and director of *The Domestic Crusaders*. She writes:

> We met Wajahat and his parents over dinner at Spenger's, a longtime Berkeley seafood restaurant. Wajahat and I found we worked well together (his interests and writing habits remind me of my husband's in many ways), and by 2004 I was directing the first staged readings at Mehran restaurant in Newark, a hub of the Bay Area's South Asian community.
>
> The play ran nearly three hours—a very long time to hold the attention of today's theatergoers, and eventually we trimmed it down to two—but the sold-out audience roared through every scene.

Thus began the journey of *The Domestic Crusaders*, and the debut of a major new talent for the American stage. The staged readings moved to Chandni—another important South Asian community gathering place in the same Newark, California, mall as Mehran—and long weekend rehearsals took place in the back garden of our Oakland home, where Wajahat's mom would send the cast homemade biryani (Wajahat's parents, Zulfiqar and Sameena Ali, have supported Wajahat's evolution as an artist all the way; their furniture has sometimes appeared as part of the set) and Wajahat himself would make chai. Carla did all the other heavy lifting; I confess I used to come down to eat biryani and check on the chaos from time to time.

And now, as the show winds its way from stage to stage and city to city, picking up admiration from critics and artists alike, I expect that my judgment, once thought to be hyperbolic, will be borne out. This play, *The Domestic Crusaders*, is the peer of those classic theatrical works that Wajahat Ali, nearly nine years ago, first used as his models.

CAST OF CHARACTERS

KHULSOOM/AMI (MOTHER)

5'4", early- to mid-fifties. Dyed-black hair, slightly long, but graying. Young looking, with wrinkles around the eyes, bags underneath. Carries herself without a slouch. Some weight around the hips, about fifteen to twenty pounds overweight but not in bad shape. Scarf around neck. Wearing traditional female shalwar khameez.

About this name: Khulsoom is a common name among Pakistani women. Umm Khulsoom was a daughter of the prophet Muhammad; she was married to the son of Abu Lahab, an uncle and later a staunch enemy of the Prophet. Abu Lahab and his son renounced her when Islam became more popular in their community, and Khulsoom eventually remarried Uthman, the third caliph. A famous story relates that when assassins came to kill the prophet Muhammad, they heard the voices of several women, including Khulsoom, from within the house. This deterred them.

FATIMA (DAUGHTER)

5'2", twenty-four years old. Hair covered by white hijab, wearing stylish red designer sweater and designer blue jeans. Green armband.

About this name: Fatima was the name of the prophet Muhammad's most beloved daughter. She is one of the most revered figures in all of Islam. Often called Fatima Az Zhara, or "the Shining Personality," she is remembered as loyal, brave, and virtuous, and is one of the four "perfected women"—the others being Khadija (the first wife of Muhammad), Mariam (Mary), and Asiya (the wife of the Egyptian pharaoh who aided Moses).

SALAHUDDIN/SAL (ELDER SON)

5'10", twenty-seven years old. Skinny, but with muscular definition. Brown/black hair. Dark black designer pants, shoes, and jacket. White, collared Banana Republic business-type shirt. Noticeable silver belt. Kind of like a suave pitbull.

About this name: Salahuddin is an uncommon name these days. Salahuddin Ayubbid, a Kurd, united Egyptian and Syrian forces to reclaim Jerusalem and temporarily stop the crusader's invasion. He was known for his ascetic personality, genial manners, cunning, and military brilliance. Under his rule, Jerusalem was quiet for three years, with peace among Christians, Jews, and Muslims. Many Muslims continue to ask, "Who will be our next Salahuddin?"

HAKIM/DAADA (GRANDFATHER)

Balding, with gray hair and gray beard. 5'7" due to slouch. Walks tall, chin up, but belly out. Strong shoulders, a man with discipline but beaten down by age. Wears a Jinnah cap and traditional white shalwar khameez. Carries a stick and *dhikr* (prayer) beads in right hand.

About this name: Many Muslim names, like this one, are derived from the "ninety-nine names of Allah"—essences or attributes of Allah mentioned in the Qu'ran. One of the meanings of Al Hakim is "the Perfectly Wise," or "the Perfect Judge." Since one cannot assume *the* name of Allah, the prefix *Abd* (slave) is often added.

SALMAN/ABU (FATHER)

5'9", late fifties. Graying hair, gradually thinning. Dark black eyes. Wearing black khaki pants, white business shirt, gray socks, and desi sandals. A reddish tint to his skin. Looks slightly haggard/tired.

About this name: Salman is a very "South Asian" version of Sulayman. The former is Urdu; the latter is Farsi. A common name for males, in this case it's based on Sulayman "the Magnificent" of Turkey, the celebrated Sultan of the Ottoman Empire during the sixteenth century. He revived the empire and started another golden era for Muslims.

GHAFUR (YOUNGER SON)

6', fit but not muscular build, light brown eyes, light black hair, fair skinned. Wearing average Western clothing, green shirt, but also a black *kufi* (Muslim skullcap).

About this name: Ghafur is another name/attribute of Allah. Al Ghafur is a very powerful name, invoking "the One Who Covers," or the "the One Who Forgives"—"the Coverer of Faults."

ACT I

TOM JONES AND
THE BIRYANI SURPRISE

TIME: *12:25 p.m., twenty-first century.*

SETTING*: Imagine an open space in a large, light-filled, contemporary suburban home, with the kitchen area (stage left) opening into the family room (stage right). There is a television in the family room, downstage of a large sofa. The kitchen has a spacious, illuminated oak floor. The refrigerator, cabinets, and sink are close to the stage-left wing. In the middle of the kitchen is the stove; a large dining table stands near it. The street lies beyond a door, stage left.*

AT RISE: *As the curtain opens, the Arabic call to prayer, the* adhan*, is heard for about sixty seconds. KHULSOOM, the mother, is cooking, preparing various dishes. She is wearing the hijab, but very loosely, showing about a quarter of her hair.*

After the adhan ends, KHULSOOM sits on a chair, raises her hands for about five seconds, and then blows on her chest and quickly rubs her hands over her face. Finished with her supplications, she goes over to the clock radio that has been playing the adhan, turns it off, and switches on the radio. Various frequencies are audible. She finally settles on an oldies station, which is broadcasting a classic by Tom Jones.

KHULSOOM: (*Taking off her hijab so that it hangs like a scarf around her neck, she sings the lyrics in accented English while rhythmically bobbing her head to the music. She's rushing around, straightening the family room.*) Hmnnn… mmm… mmmmmm… to be loved by anyone… Ta-da da da… It's not *unusual* to be… hmmmn… mmmm… mmm… happens every day… la la la la…

FATIMA: (*In hijab, speaking American English with something like a Valley Girl accent*) Ugh, I hear *old* people music. Ami, puhlease, *please*—*anything* but Tom Jones.

KHULSOOM: (*Annoyed*) *Oy, chup!*[1] I have to listen to all this gangster-rap music all you kids listen to—all killing! (*Makes a pistol with her fist and fingers*) Bang. Bang. *Dishoom.* Shoot this, shoot him, shoot that… Doggy dogg, Puffy bakwas, nonsense. At least this music—the words I can understand—

(*FATIMA tries to change the radio. Her mom has her back turned.*)

KHULSOOM: *Khabardar,*[2] Fatima. Don't even *think* of changing Tom.

FATIMA: Great, you're on a first-name basis with him now.

KHULSOOM: Your daadi, Allah bless her soul, couldn't get enough of him. Remember—

FATIMA: Yes, yes, yes—you've told us a thousand times. When you and grandmother first came here, Abu took you all to the Tom Jones concert. You and grandmother, in your shalwar khameez and dupatta, the only desi FOBs there—

---

[1] "Hey, be quiet!"
[2] "Beware"

3

KHULSOOM: That's right—we wore our clothes. And why not? Your ami is an FOB and proud of it. Fresh... Fresh on the... what is it?

FATIMA: Fresh Off the Boat!

KHULSOOM: *Hanh*,[3] well, at least us FOBs were wearing something. All those *nangay*, naked hippie women throwing their panties, *astaghfirullah*.[4] (*Shakes her head disapprovingly, lightly taps both cheeks twice*)

FATIMA: (*Disgusted*) Okay, ami. Please. Never use the word *panties* again. (*Shudders*) It's just not right to hear that coming from your mouth.

KHULSOOM: Oh, sorry—I forgot your Ami is some backward, uneducated, *ghown*, village woman, hay na?[5] (*Imitates a stereotypical South Asian woman, placing a bowl on her head, walking with hand on her hips—FATIMA laughs.*) Us FOBs aren't as slow as you think, Missy. We can teach you Amreekans a thing or two about—

FATIMA: Okay, okay, you win, Ms. FOB 2010.

KHULSOOM: Hmph. Now, be useful. Drop those law books—learn something *practical*—come here, wear that apron. I bought it just for you. Grab the tamatar, hari mirch, and pyaaz from the fridge. You'll make the raita for Ghafur's biryani. He'll be so happy his sister helped make some food for him on his birthday.

FATIMA: He *definitely* won't eat it if he knows I made it. Even *I* wouldn't eat it. (*KHULSOOM looks at FATIMA, who looks back. Eventually, she sighs.*) Fine. One condition, though. I get to change this atrocious song.

---

[3] "Yes"
[4] "may Allah forgive me"
[5] "right?"

(KHULSOOM snarls, and then throws her hand in the air in assent. FATIMA changes the radio, finally settling on an AM news station. Once her choice is made, she goes to the fridge, opens it, and stares, obviously not able to find the vegetables.)

RADIO: *(Voice-over)* We now return to our in-depth coverage of "The War against Extremism." Joining us now for an NPR exclusive are world-renowned, respected academic experts on Islam and the Middle East—

(FATIMA, visibly disgusted, turns it off)

FATIMA: *(To no one)* Experts! What a joke.

KHULSOOM: Pathetic! You don't even know where the onions are! How do you expect me to teach you how to cook if you can't find the onions in your own house?

FATIMA: Well, this is *not* my house. This is *your* house. I only come on the weekends—

KHULSOOM: Yeah, come on the weekends to give me your dirty laundry and your empty food trays. Trays that I fill every week with *my* food—

FATIMA: Yeah, and I eat it. I'm grateful, all right? I didn't *say* anything. Besides—I don't even want to learn how to cook. I don't care if—

KHULSOOM: *(Exasperated)* Chup! *(Puts her index finger to her lips)* Second tray from the bottom. Bring the onions. Here, cut them the way I taught you.

(KHULSOOM hands FATIMA an intimidating knife. FATIMA, the Padawan, stares at it with apprehension and fear. KHULSOOM, the Jedi Kitchen Master, stands over her, inspecting her every move. FATIMA wields the

knife in the most ungraceful, humorous fashion. KHULSOOM grows increasingly irritated with each cut her apprentice makes. Finally—)

KHULSOOM: Ya, Allah! Here, move. I'll do it.

(*KHULSOOM completes the task with amazing, exaggerated speed, then combines the chopped vegetables in a single dish, adding some lemon sauce, some pepper, some salt. She hands a simple serving spoon to FATIMA.*)

KHULSOOM: Now all you have to do is stir. Think you can manage that, Ms. Barrister?

FATIMA: (*Sarcastically*) Yes, I can manage that. (*Not really doing as her mother requests, as it will be throughout the day*) Sorry if some of us have other things to do in life besides learning how to cook desi food, Ami. Sorry if learning to cook for my future husband isn't my number-one priority. Sorry if I'm not "well-trained, Muslim desi housewife" material—

KHULSOOM: (*More calmly*) Beti, you are young and headstrong—*like your father*. It has nothing to do with being a trained, Muslim, desi housewife. Inshallah, you'll learn that the way to please a man—and a family—is through gentleness and good food. Treating your husband with respect doesn't make you a slave. I'll tell you a secret all wise women know: feed your man well with good food every night, and he'll never chase after another woman. Also, he won't mind if you gain the pounds here and there. (*Playfully pinches FATIMA's hips*)

FATIMA: Ami, for the last time, I really don't care what "men" like. Muslim men are all boorish, sexually frustrated, horny juveniles. Plus, we all know they don't like "a good Muslim girl who can

6

cook." All these FOB guys want is (*in one breath*) a good Muslim girl with *light* skin tone, an *MD* degree, long hair, *stunning* looks, among her other *assets*, and who *must* cook like their *mother*. Life doesn't revolve around marriage. Tell that to your gossipy aunty squad.

KHULSOOM: Tell them that on top of what they, and Allah knows who else, has already heard of you? My only beti, twenty-four years old. *Still* single! No proposals from anyone. Instead of attending her law-school classes, goes to these rallies. Once such a nice girl, now wearing hijab, giving controversial speeches, getting arrested at the university protest, going out on the town with *blacks*—

FATIMA: Okay! Can we get over this already? Who cares? It's not a big deal! And (*in a South Asian accent*) the "blaycks" are people, too— they're Muslim! Remember, no color barrier in the religion? You guys are so—so—obtuse! There are more important things than my stupid "bio-data marriage application."

KHULSOOM: You better mind your place, larki—watch your tongue! Your parents aren't (*in a Valley Girl accent*) "obtuse"—we just look out for you because—

(*SAL, KHULSOOM's eldest child, has walked in, unnoticed, as the situation becomes increasingly volatile. He listens for a few seconds, then hums the "1812 Overture" and strolls around, trying to appear oblivious to the argument. When he stops humming, the women stop talking, and both stare at him.*)

SAL: The battle of the hijabi versus the non-hijabi, round one! And in this corner, we have, wearing a lovely scarf—

(*The women roll their eyes, but can't contain their laughter. The tension lessens.*)

FATIMA: Sal, you are a *perennial* ten-year-old. Grow up.

SAL: Whoa, whoa. Easy, *Webster's Dictionary*. Not all of us corporate drones understand your big words.

KHULSOOM: (*Half-smiling*) Salu. When will you grow up? Go find a nice girl, give me some grandchildren—*quickly*, and move back to the house so I can play with them.

SAL: Ami, you know I find nice girls all the time.

KHULSOOM: Find *one* nice girl, oh *badmash*![6]

SAL: Then what? Who will cook me *khana*?[7] Look at Fatima—none of these girls know how to cook.

(*FATIMA scowls at him.*)

SAL: And no one cooks biryani and tandoori chicken like my *ami jaan*.[8] Plus, American girls can't get along with the mother-in-law. Clash of Civilizations. Can't move back to the house due to conflict of interests.

KHULSOOM: Well, you should! He misses you, you know. We all do.

SAL: (*Obviously not convinced*) Riiiiight.

KHULSOOM: (*Playfully*) You don't even like my khana. You never have. Always munching on McDonald's burgers and fries. (*Grabs his ear and tugs it*) Such terrible food. I pray your wife makes you start liking desi cooking!

FATIMA: What wife?

---

[6] "scoundrel"
[7] "food"
[8] "beloved mother"

KHULSOOM: And I pray your wife—your future wife (*says* "Ameen"[9] *under her breath twice*)—isn't twisted in the head with all these liberated MTV thoughts of having "*my own space.*" You find one that has strong family ties and traditions.

SAL: I'll find the best *bahu*[10] for you, Ami. Don't you worry. She'll be 5'9", fit and trim, nice, healthy body—

(*KHULSOOM and FATIMA shake their heads.*)

SAL: —with a (*in an Indian accent*) "green card" and fair and lovely skin tone. And plus, Ami, you know I love your chicken, but you know how it is with me and the spices (*rubs stomach*)—gives me gas. Plus bad breath.

FATIMA: (*Quietly, in a mocking tone to SAL, so KHULSOOM cannot hear*) Then why don't you use a breath mint before you start talking to all those greasy *gorees*[11] and European girls you always try to befriend? *Try*, I repeat, to befriend.

SAL: Whoa, whoa, easy there, Paki McBeal! Why the sudden angst and rage? What—the hijab wrapped a little too tight today, huh? (*Knocks on her head*) Upset there's no protest today? Actually have to do work and be useful? Say, I've got a classic idea. I'll make costumes for you and your radical ninja "sisters," with a big *M* smack-dab in the middle—kind of like Superman but more lame. And more fundamentalist. That way you guys can stop those bombs in *style*. (*Does a ninja pose*)

---

[9] "Amen"
[10] "daughter-in-law"
[11] "white women"

FATIMA: (*Very fast, sassy delivery*) Ha-ha—very funny, "*Sal.*" I'm glad someone who spends all his time thinking about cheap, ho-ey white girls—the ones he can never have, by the way—and the stock market, and his gaudy new Versace belt (*points to the big, conspicuous* V *on SAL's belt*), probably made by some poor eight-year-old refugee in a third-world labor camp, can lecture me on *my* activities. I can't believe you don't even care your people are being senselessly massacred.

SAL: (*Raises eyebrows*) My people?

FATIMA: Yes, your people! You should be there with me, and with my "sisters," who by the way are known as muhajjabahs, and should be respected because they have the modesty to cover themselves in order to keep away from Studio 54 rejects like you.

SAL: (*Coolly*) I got into Studio 54—Las Vegas. And please, *please*—keep me and all sane heterosexual men as far away from your insane, jihadi penguin squad (*FATIMA touches her hijab*) as possible. Seriously, those girls need to wise up and stop com*plaining*. Wasting your time on this newfound Muslim Justice League—(*trying to find right words*) crusader fad—phase. Are we the same girl who went to the prom with *En-ri-que* San-chez, the high-school running back?

FATIMA: That was a *long* time ago. Give me a break. And plus, I didn't even *do* anything. You're the one who gets away with everything.

KHULSOOM: Don't talk of these things. Always fight-—

SAL: Typical Muslims—blame America for *every*thing. Whine, whine, whine, nag, nag, nag. Listen up, Hij-Abbie Hoffman—people are still dying, just like they always have, and just like they always will. Enjoy it while you can, sis. It's all going to hell soon enough.

FATIMA: Well, I guess some of us don't have the privilege of being content with our apathy.

SAL: Why don't you lecture your feminazi fundo "sisters" about spending all their carefree time doing something useful—like learning how to cook? Or going to the gym? Maybe, *maybe* then they might trick some poor, blind FOB into proposing so he can get his visa—that's of course before they swell up like a naan after the marriage. (*Inflates his cheeks and raises arms around his stomach*)

FATIMA: Oh my God! I can't *believe* you just said that, Sal! I swear I'm going to kill you! (*Punches him in the arm*)

KHULSOOM: Chup! Enough! I don't want to hear it. And Fatima, be obedient to your older brother! (*She raises both her arms to signify the end of the conversation. FATIMA is flustered, as usual, that her mom sides with SAL.*) Today is Ghafur's twenty-first birthday, and I don't want him to hear yelling when he comes into the kitchen. This is the first time in months my children and family are all together under the same roof—just like the old times. I won't have your bickering ruin it! (*Looks at both her children*) Okay?!

(*They grumble in acquiescence.*)

SAL: Ami, I swear you're like some third-world dictator of the kitchen. It's not even cool. I feel like I'm in China.

KHULSOOM: Call me Mao. Now go set the table with your sister.

SAL: (*A half smile, shaking his head*) Fine. Fine. You win! I can't believe a twenty-seven-year-old man is being told how to live his life by his mother. Only in a Muslim Pakistani family, I swear.

FATIMA: (*In agreement*) Seriously.

KHULSOOM: Yeah, well, I didn't ask to have these love handles, either, so go set the table and don't talk back to me. *Yeh pagal bachay koy thameez nahee, ya adab... thoba...*[12]

(*FATIMA interrupts her rant*)

FATIMA: How come Abu hasn't come down yet?

KHULSOOM: (*Slightly annoyed, but worried*) He isn't here.

SAL: (*Muttering audibly under his breath*) Thank god.

KHULSOOM: (*Pretending not to hear*) He didn't come home all night.

FATIMA: What? Is he okay? I thought you all were sleeping when I came in last night.

KHULSOOM: Yes, yes—it's just some deadline for some project his team is doing. He's been working day and night—*pagalohn kay jaisay*,[13] like crazy. That's why he's one of the lead engineers, you know—(*saying this to SAL, with some pride*) a chief manager on this pipeline project. He's excited, says he might have some *good news* for us—

SAL: Faaaan-tastic.

KHULSOOM: (*Coaxing*) Why don't you call him, Beta? See when he's coming? He'd like that.

SAL: I—forgot his number. And plus—he'd want his favorite to call him, right? (*Pointing to FATIMA*)

---

[12] "These crazy kids today—no manners, etiquette, respect... terrible"
[13] "like a madman"

12

FATIMA: Oh, I'm *so* not his favorite. You and Ghafur always say that, you know it's not true—

(Cell-phone music is heard—the really annoying kind. It's SAL's phone. SAL closes his eyes as if he's been caught red-handed, then quickly improvises.)

SAL: Oh. *(Looks at the screen, smiles)* It's a miracle! *(He looks at the sky, then silences his cell phone.)* Sorry, urgent call from work. Guess dishes duty is up to you, Fatima. I really am torn, I do want to stay and help you, truly I do—but business is business.

FATIMA: *(Perturbed)* Yeah, tell *her* I said salaams… or namaste… or moshi moshi… or shalom!

(At the last one SAL looks back quickly, realizes FATIMA was just kidding, and the panic that has suddenly risen in his face vanishes, replaced by a smirk. He exits stage left.)

KHULSOOM: That boy… I just… I don't know what…

FATIMA: What? Oh, don't worry—I'll call Abu—

KHULSOOM: *(In the midst of cooking)* It's not that—well, it is that also, but— my first-born child… *(Shakes her head)* My daughter, my children… *(Sighs)* They all blame me. Mothers are blamed for everything— always. You always have to sacrifice something to come out clean in the end. Remember that when you have little ones, Fatima.

FATIMA: I… have… *no idea* what that just meant, but I'll be sure to tell the "little ones" immediately—right as soon as they pop out of the womb. Won't be happening for a long time, though.

KHULSOOM: Anyway, call your father. Tell him he has to come in the next hour or he's not getting any food. Hanh, tell him that. He'll come running. And your grandfather should be coming down any second. (*Annoyed*) And go wake up Ghafur—tell that elephant he can't sleep all day.

FATIMA: (*Yells*) Ghafur, get up!

KHULSOOM: *I* could've done that, Fatima. I told you to *go* and wake him. No use. Pathetic. Finish setting the table.

FATIMA: What am I, Aunt Mammy the slave girl?

KHULSOOM: Yes, now do as I say and do it quick.

FATIMA: (*Grudgingly*) Yes, massa. Yes, massa.

KHULSOOM: Ghafur, *neechay ow*![14] Ghafur, wake up, you elephant! Ghafur…

(*Her voice trails off as the lights fade.*)

---

[14] "Come downstairs"

SCENE II
BIG TROUBLE
IN LITTLE KABUL

TIME: *1 p.m.*

SETTING: *Family room/kitchen.*

AT RISE: *The scene begins in darkness. As the lights come up, we see HAKIM, the paternal grandfather, entering the kitchen from the foot of the stairs. He has a paper under his arm and is walking with a cane. FATIMA and KHULSOOM are still in the kitchen, preparing the meal.*

HAKIM: (*Booming voice, deep*) Assalam Alikum!

FATIMA: Slaleekoom, Daada.

KHULSOOM: (*Regroups*) Slaleekoom, Dad.

(*FATIMA goes to her grandfather, bows, and burrows herself in his chest to give him a hug.*)

HAKIM: Wa laikum. How is my rani doing? (*Kisses her on her cheek, with a boisterous smile*)

FATIMA: *Alhamdulilah.*[15] (*Goes back to help KHULSOOM. HAKIM has seated himself on the couch in the family room.*)

HAKIM: I thought I heard the adhan?

FATIMA: Yeah, the entire neighborhood heard it… followed naturally by Tom Jones. Doesn't matter, all the neighbors think we're freaks, anyway. I heard the kids next door complain that our house smells like Little Kabul.

KHULSOOM: Kya? Kabul? We're not those *Afghanis*. We're *Pakistanis!* Why don't you tell them, Fatima? I've lived here long enough. They should at least give respect and know who I am. At least not call me some Afghani.

FATIMA: Yeah, Ami. Do you think trailer-trash Bob and his Podunk wife know the difference?

HAKIM: Close—close enough. Afghanistan is next to Pakistan, and they are Muslims. They didn't call us Mexican. Or Sikhs, ha! Should be grateful.

FATIMA: Exactly. They probably think we're Hindu or something.

HAKIM: Yesterday at the flea market, I was picking my fruits—as usual. One white man was next to me. He was with his son—just a boy, probably eight or so. The boy looked up at me and asked, "Are you related to Osama bin Laden?"

FATIMA: What? No way!

---

[15] "Glory be to God."

HAKIM: Hanh, I heard it. My own ears—and *Allah thera shukar*[16] I'm not deaf yet.

KHULSOOM: What did you tell him? I would have said, "Yes, yes I am."

HAKIM: You want to get your father-in-law arrested, Beti? He's just a kid—I said no, no, I'm not. *He* is a terrorist who doesn't know the first thing about the religion of Islam. *I* am a proud Musalman, Alhamdulilah, born and raised in Hyderabad Deccan, India.

FATIMA: (*Sarcastically*) Yeah, way to go, I'm sure he processed all that.

HAKIM: Then, after all this, the boy asks, "Do you speak Hindu?" Do *I* speak *Hindu?*

FATIMA: This should have been recorded. It's classic—

HAKIM: Hmph, classic. I wanted to slap him for his ignorance, but his father was right there. These children… little devils. If I would have said that to an old man at that age and my father was there, oof! A*ik thappar*[17] would come flying down. But I knew he meant well. Heh, just a *bacha*, a kid. So I said, "No, no, I don't speak Hindu, little one. But I do speak Muslimonics." (*Chuckles to himself*) I gave him a toffee to make him happy, but I don't think he got the joke.

KHULSOOM: Well, as long as they don't call us Little Kabul, I don't care. I mean, at least Little Karachi, or Little Islamabad—even Little Bombay, or Little Delhi, but no Kabul! These Afghanis, they all come here on asylum, taking the government's money, sitting cozy.

---

[16] "Thank Allah"
[17] "One slap"

The *mujahideen bicharay*[18] all got left behind, but no, no, all the rest came here on *asylum*.

FATIMA: You're just angry because first they go to Pakistan and get all the pretty girls and guys.

KHULSOOM: I'm angry because they let the Taliban take over their country, and they did nothing. Let the U.S. bomb these bicharay children, these poor women in Afghanistan—and what? Nothing.

FATIMA: Oh, yeah, we're ones to talk. What did we do? How many did anything? How many Muslims protested the Taliban? What did you do? Exactly. And if you have all this hate for them, how come you care they get bombed?

KHULSOOM: You and your... your law talk and theatrics. All questions and arguments. No one *hates* them. I don't hate them, thoba. They are Muslims. They are Muslims—but they're not Pakistani! And, as I was saying, we don't even look the same.

FATIMA: Close enough. All you guys look alike.

HAKIM: But, mashallah, their food is excellent! Chapali kebob and boolani—subhanallah! Brilliant!

KHULSOOM: Well, today we will have lamb biryani for your brother's birthday. Inshallah, God willing, when Ghafur becomes the rich and famous surgeon doctor he can hire a maasi maid to cook biryani for *me* for a change.

HAKIM: And a maalish to massage my back.

---

[18] "poor freedom fighters"

FATIMA: When he actually gets into a medical school, Dr. Ghafur can find himself a stunning *light* skin tone, white but not *white* Kashmiri girl who makes biryani like it was manna from heaven.

KHULSOOM: Inshallah! But don't give the evil eye to your brother. I don't want him jinxed.

HAKIM: Well, let me give an evil eye to this biryani. I don't think it will mind. (*Closes eyes and inhales*)

(*HAKIM walks over to smell the biryani, putting his arm around KHULSOOM. He begins walking back to the family room. SAL enters and sits in his father's family-room chair, adjacent to the couch. He sifts through the paper, picking up the business section.*)

SAL: About time, been sitting on that stock for weeks.

HAKIM: (*Stares at SAL for a moment—then coughs, then coughs again*) Oy, *bandar!*[19] What kind of badtameez disrespectful man doesn't say salaams to his own grandfather!

SAL: Uh, oh, sorry, Daada. You know, just, uh, lost in thoughts is all. Salaams. (*Hesitates, goes to him, tries to bow like FATIMA, doesn't really succeed*) Just that—um—had a call from work. I'll probably have to leave early today—arrange the initial seeds of a possible merger. You know the life. Always moving. (*Snaps fingers*) Sorry, Ami.

KHULSOOM: (*Snaps her fingers in response*) What is this leaving early? You should be ashamed! Your brother is here after a long time, the family is together, but *now* we have more important commitments than our family? Khalaas—cancel it.

---

[19] "monkey"

SAL: But—I—

KHULSOOM: (*Raises eyebrows*) Salahuddin—can—cel—it.

SAL: Yeah, we'll see. Let's move this already. Come on. Wake that kid up. (*HAKIM is once again seated on the couch.*)

HAKIM: Sal, your father will be down any second. (*Motioning him to move*)

SAL: I know, I know. I'll move when—if—he gets here.

HAKIM: In the meantime, give me my *dhood* with *shahed* and some *khajoors*.

FATIMA: Honey with milk and dates every day—same routine for as long as I can remember.

HAKIM: Forty-five years, Beti.

(*HAKIM's eyes drift off for a bit. SAL gets up, grudgingly, but only after KHULSOOM has already given her father-in-law his milk, dates, and honey on a tray.*)

HAKIM: Thank you, Beta.

(*SAL gets up and sits next to HAKIM on the sofa.*)

SAL: Yeah, sorry, um. So, uh, is it true?

HAKIM: Is what true?

(*As HAKIM pours the honey into his milk, SAL leans closer to his grandfather, his tone hushed, a little surreptitious.*)

SAL: The old wives' tale—I mean, the old… scholars and Sufis, what they say—about dates with milk and honey and how it… umm…

helps man in his various, um, spiritual and *physical* conditions.

HAKIM: (*In a commanding, grandfatherly tone*) These are the traditions of the prophet Muhammad, peace be upon him! Honey, the blessed nectar of paradise, as mentioned in the Qu'ran. Dates, the blessed fruit of Medina, city of the prophet Muhammad *salalaho alayhi wa salam*.[20] And milk, the Prophet's favorite drink! When given a choice between water, wine, and milk, the Prophet chose milk because it was the moderate choice. The middle path.

SAL: Yeah, yeah, great. Middle path. *Awesome*. And what about the whole *physical* part? You know, how it supposedly helps man in his… *activities?*

HAKIM: (*Slowly looks at SAL*) And it doesn't hurt in that department either.

(*SAL, upon hearing this, voraciously stuffs four dates into his mouth, and downs a glass of milk with some honey.*)

HAKIM: Though Allah has made everything with a definite purpose and limitation. Sometimes, no matter how much we water our plant, it will never increase in *size* or *strength*.

(*HAKIM chuckles and opens up his newspaper. SAL looks anguished. He spits the remnants of his food into a napkin. FATIMA reads her book, stirring the pot in a most uninterested fashion. KHULSOOM is excited, running about preparing the meal. SAL yells for GHAFUR to come down.*)

SAL: Ghafur! I'm gonna hurt you if you don't come down here…

(*The lights go down in the kitchen.*)

---

[20] "may peace be upon him." Often added out of respect after a mention of the Prophet's name.

A MAN PREFERS SYMMETRY

TIME: *Five minutes later.*

SETTING: *We are now focused on the family room. We see a nice chair stage right of the sofa; it "belongs" to SALMAN, the father. A small, embroidered couch is to the right of the chair, and another is to the left of the sofa. There is an elegant Middle Eastern coffee table on a beautiful carpet in the middle of the room, with magazines and the TV remote on top, and a variety of papers on the bottom shelf. Shoes are lined up perfectly by the door, away from the carpet. There is a small desk near the kitchen area, and a brass or carved-wood coat rack by the entryway.*

AT RISE: *SALMAN enters, slightly stooped, wearing his business clothes: white business shirt, black khakis. He is obviously perturbed about something, and looks a little haggard. No one hears him returning home. He puts down his*

*briefcase, takes off his jacket and hangs it up, then loosens his tie and changes
from street shoes to chapals, all while reading the front page of the newspaper.*

SALMAN: Tired of this goddamn heat… Goddamn media. Same nonsense
every day! Blame Islam. Blame Muslims. Blame immigrants for
everything! Tired of the daily propaganda!

*(SALMAN turns on the television almost immediately after he enters the house.
He crosses the room, picks up the remote, and clicks through a few channels. He
goes past Fox News, disgusted, and lands on a talking-head commentator. He
mutters to himself.)*

SALMAN: So, Iran is making weapons now? Why don't you tell us
who sold it to them in the first place!? *Jhootay! Haramzaday!*[21]
Who's that? Right—another Amreekan general telling me why the
Muslim world hates us. Amreeka, everyone is an expert—(*The rest
of the family is illuminated now, aware of his rant*) morons, absolute
idiots, liars, liars running this country, the worthless media, the oil
companies—Muslims—useless also—stabbing you in the back—

SAL: And so it begins.

FATIMA: Salaams to you too, Abu. (*FATIMA goes over to her father, and he
kisses her.*)

SALMAN: Sorry, Beti. Salaams. (*He cools down.*)

KHULSOOM: You look terrible—did you sleep? Did you even eat? Why
were you there all night? You didn't even answer your cell. And
your pants, how come they're wet? Did you step in some puddles?

---

[21] "Liars! Bastards!"

SALMAN: (*Flustered*) Just—uh—everything is fine. I ate. I ate. I slept—don't worry. Just some puddles. You're right. You're *always* right. (*Forces a smile*) Good, good you came this weekend.

(*SALMAN gives FATIMA a hug, and another kiss on her forehead, and his mood becomes more pleasant. Referring to her hijab, he comments—*)

SALMAN: Abey, no need to wear this in the house? We're all family men—you can take it off. You have such nice hair. I miss seeing it.

FATIMA: I have a bad-hair day today, and I have to go out later—

(*As FATIMA fixes her hijab, KHULSOOM, the non-hijabi, gives her a look, and SALMAN chuckles. He bends down in traditional South Asian fashion and places his head near his father's stomach. HAKIM places his hand on his son's head.*)

HAKIM: (*Smiling*) Jeetay raho, jeetay raho.[22]

(*There is an awkward pause. SAL has returned to SALMAN's chair, oblivious of his father's hovering presence.*)

HAKIM: (*Sharply*) Salahuddin! Your father's chair.

SAL: Of course, the royal throne. How dare I? (*Picks up his magazine, uncomfortably walks away from his father toward the kitchen, muttering*) Salaams.

SALMAN: Hmph. Salaams. (*Muttering audibly*) Probably ran out of food this month. (*SAL ignores his comments. SALMAN shakes his head, then suddenly starts sniffing.*) Khulsoom, I smell biryani. Kya, is it chick—

---

[22] "Keep living, keep living."

KHULSOOM: Now, don't you begin with me, too. It's not chicken, it's lamb. And all you're thinking about is food—typical men. Look at you, you look like—like a—

SAL: A waste.

KHULSOOM: —some tired *boodha*.[23] Why don't you go rest? Arey, at least go freshen up.

(*KHULSOOM fusses over SALMAN like mothers do with their children. He rebels like children and husbands often do, with pained expressions and arm movements meant to get her away.*)

SALMAN: *Choro. Khana nikaalo.*[24] I'll be fresh if I eat. I'm starving. Did you say lamb? (*Annoyed*) Hunh? I keep telling you not to make lamb biryani, yet you insist on making lamb biryani when you know I don't prefer it! No one in this house eats it.

KHULSOOM: *Everyone* in this house eats lamb, except you and your stubborn daughter.

FATIMA: Hey, wait, how'd I get caught in this fight?

SALMAN: No one is fighting. It's just the last fifty times, all we've had is lamb biryani. Your mother has forgotten how to cook anything else. Hay na, Baba?

HAKIM: (*Drops newspaper*) Beta, I'm an old man. Don't get me involved. I just thank Allah that she still puts food on my plate, and that I still have the teeth to eat it. Alhamdulilah.

---

[23] "old man"
[24] "Leave it. Take out the food"

KHULSOOM: Your wife hasn't forgotten anything! The last three parties we went to, they just happened to have served lamb biryani, remember? Kashif's shaadi last week? Mumtaz's dinner the week before?

SALMAN: Oh—her? The one who wears all that makeup all the time?

KHULSOOM: Yeah, that one. She's gone—(*in a very thick accent*) "bee-lond" now.

SALMAN: Hanh, the "bee-lond" one I remember. Hanh, that one—last week's—you just said it—his name I forgot—married the Jewish girl.

KHULSOOM: Kashif and Elaine.

SALMAN: Sha! *Elaine*. Of all the girls—couldn't find *one* decent Muslim one. Anyway, they can't even spend enough money to cater edible food. You'd think they would—married a Jew and all. Food probably wasn't even Halal—lied about it. Probably wasn't even Kosher, either. Considering *Elaine* doesn't look like the Hasidic Jew—

FATIMA: Or act like it.

KHULSOOM: If they said it was Halal—it's Halal. His mother is particular on it. They wouldn't feed us unkoshered meat.

SALMAN: Well, she obviously isn't *too* particular—lets her only son marry a Jewish girl. Not even a pretty one, at that.

SAL: So what if she's Jewish? Who cares?

HAKIM: (*Shrugs*) They are... People of the Book, Allah has said it is lawful to marry their women. They believe in Allah and the Last Day, but... they just—

FATIMA: Hate our people? Oppress Palestinians? Own Hollywood, distort the media?

HAKIM: (*Grimaces*) Just—they have never respected us and our ways—they will never... adopt our customs and beliefs. Best would have been to convert her to Islam first, or not marry her at all.

SAL: Great—I'm listening to anti-Semites in my house. Unleash the swastikas!

SALMAN: Wait just a minute—hold on—I'm not an anti-Semite. This country conveniently calls us anti-Semites anytime we criticize Israel for anything. I don't hate the Jews or Judaism. I'm just *saying* that it's not *wise* to marry a *girl* like *that*, especially when you have such nice Muslim girls—like Fatima—(*she rolls her eyes*) around who are just the same, if not better. Muslim men—they don't think with their head. They think with something else, these days.

KHULSOOM: So sad. And what about the kids? Muslim or Jewish? Probably neither—they'll be so confused. Become atheists and druggies after the divorce.

SALMAN: Some mutant combination. They'll be called Mu-Jews.

FATIMA: Jeez—don't be too optimistic, now. Inshallah, I *hope* they don't divorce. They seem happy, and they like each other. That's what counts, in the end. It's his choice, even though it is... an unattractive one.

SAL: Well, *I* don't see anything wrong with it at all. Doesn't matter if she's Jewish, Christian, vegan, or whatever. He loves her, she loves him. End of story. So what if they aren't hard-core? Probably it'll work out for the best. (*Looks to FATIMA*) Their kids won't be poisoned with deranged propaganda, at least. Heck—who knows, I might find *me* a nice Jewish girl!

KHULSOOM: Salahuddin! Do thoba now! (*She starts saying an Arabic prayer, bites her tongue, lightly taps her cheeks.*) Don't take out a bad tongue, the angels always surround us, who knows when they say Ameen!

FATIMA: (*To SAL*) You'd probably let your wife teach your kids that the Palestinians are rock-throwing terrorists. And every Arab kid is a potential ticking human time bomb. And the Israelis (*in a baby-like voice*) *obviously* are poor, defenseless innocents who just happen to have one of the world's strongest militaries, nuclear capabilities, M16s, and Apache helicopters thanks to direct support from your United States of America!

SAL: I'd teach 'em that both of 'em are nuts!

FATIMA: Not surprising.

SALMAN: (*Oblivious*) I mean, if she was pretty, I'd somewhat understand. Man likes beauty. But she's so… plain. And bland. Yoghurty. No symmetry.

KHULSOOM: Of course—only if she is pretty. The White Hourain sent from heaven, beguiling with her light-skinned beauty. With her *bee-lond* hair and blue eyes—so beautiful compared to the dark-haired, dark-skinned woman. We're just boring and common, like daily naan—nothing mysterious about us. No reason to respect us, or treat *us* like a princess. But—oh, no—when Ms. Goree *bee-lond* woman comes, (*mimicking*) *then* there comes the combed hair, the suit and tie, the wide smile with the white teeth showing. May I open the door for you, Ms. White Hourain? May I get you your food, Ms. White Hourain? May I light your cigarette, Ms. White Hourain? All of you colonized men—all the same with your hypocrisy!

SALMAN: No one has ever colonized me! Speak for yourself and your own people—Punjabis! Just because I happened to acknowledge beauty does not mean I'm a black white man with insecurity problems like these idiot, elitist doctors who throw their parties—your friends! They're the ones who'll sell their own mother to be accepted by the white man.

HAKIM: Their ancestors sold more than that when the British first came.

KHULSOOM: Yeah, they sold their pride! And they sold their respect for their women—which they never had in the first place.

SALMAN: Bah! All this feminist nonsense. You're watching too much *Oprah* and reading too many *Cosmo*s. Listen, men are disrespectful to *all* women—regardless of color. We don't discriminate! (*Chuckles*)

FATIMA: Unfortunately.

HAKIM: It's true, Bahu. Our men are in such a rush to become white and Amreekan we've forgotten our own traditions, and our own precious jewels—our women.

FATIMA: That's exactly it. People treat us like "jewels"—like we're some sort of commodity to be traded on the stock market.

SAL: Too bad your IPO hasn't gone public.

FATIMA: Ha-ha. We all know that *your* stock has been bought and sold by many shareholders.

SAL: Hey, mashallah. A bull stock—what can I say?

SALMAN: (*Trying to change the subject*) Hanh, so when is our beti going to go "public"?

FATIMA: Listen, let's *not* get into this.

SAL: (*Egging her on*) I think this is a perfect time to get into this, isn't it?

HAKIM: It's up to Fatima. But talking of such matters doesn't hurt, at times.

KHULSOOM: Talking is all we've been doing, and nothing more! Mumtaz and Kashif's friend, that Zeeshan, remember? They all came over to our house three years ago for Fatima's twenty-first birthday.

FATIMA: Yeah, and?

KHULSOOM: He was quite handsome, mashallah, a successful doctor, and he's young!

FATIMA: Ami, he's thirty-five! And *we are not* getting into this again.

KHULSOOM: Oh, chup. I'm not getting into anything. What's wrong with him, anyway?

SALMAN: Hmn, hanh, I remember him. A charming man. Educated, intelligent. A little dark, but I liked him. He's making really good money now. Stable job. Parents aren't Hyderabadi—

KHULSOOM: Or Punjabi, unfortunately.

SALMAN: Thank Allah!

KHULSOOM: Abey, *teri beevi eh Punjabi*—your wife is a Punjabi. And proud.

SALMAN: (*To his father, joking*) Look what a headache that got me. What, Fatima is interested in him? He's a good match for you. Intellectually he can challenge you, Beti.

FATIMA: God help me.

SALMAN: Just consider him as an option. An option. Your parents know you better than you know yourself.

HAKIM: Is he religious?

FATIMA: No!

KHULSOOM: Don't say that. I see him at the masjid on Fridays during Jumaa prayer. He comes from a good home.

FATIMA: Yeah, Ami. Everyone and their mother goes to Jumaa prayers on Friday. Everyone from alcoholic, Qu'ran-spouting Doctor Uncle to skanky, sixteen-year-old hoochie mamas. You and Abu think just because a Muslim girl or this guy, this Zeeshan dork doctor, goes to prayer, smiles that fake plastic smile at parties, and comes from a "good family," that they're all pious. Yeah, *right*. Their parents are so gullible. They think they're raising little angels, when those kids really go clubbing and binge-drinking every Saturday night. I refuse to succumb to that insincere, plastic nonsense, and I'm hated.

SALMAN: No one hates you, Beti.

FATIMA: Yes, they do! The aunties all whisper behind my back—at that wedding—backbiting like they always do, because I wear the hijab and they just stick some tissue paper on their heads when they hear the call to prayer at parties. They can't stand it that I'm actually making something out of my life instead of becoming an obese, wrinkled, backbiting gossip hag.

KHULSOOM: Now, wait just a second, Missy—

FATIMA: No, *you* wait. You sit there and support their little network by complaining about me and my "activities" and how I'm so picky about my husband—and then these women who have nothing better to do set up these completely ridiculous "matches" without even asking me!

KHULSOOM: Don't use that tone with me! And I told you to stop disrespecting your elders, especially your aunties. They do nothing but pray for you—and Ghafur—and Salahuddin—

SAL: They send me their *curses!* (*Muttering*) Old witches, they just never seem to die.

KHULSOOM: No one wastes their time making gossip about you. I don't tell them—

FATIMA: Yeah, sure you don't—that's why they just happen to know that I was given a warning by the school not to protest? They just happen to find out about the police, or about *Aziz*—

KHULSOOM: (*KHULSOOM's voice rises—and, slamming the knife down on the table as she cuts, she replies*) I told you we will not discuss him again! It's over and done with! Khalaas! Khatam!

FATIMA: Yeah, for you!

KHULSOOM: What does that mean?

FATIMA: (*Turns her back*) God, I'm so disgusted.

(SALMAN walks over to his daughter and puts his arm around her.)

SALMAN: Beti, relax, relax. Your mother just gets excited, you know that. *(To KHULSOOM)* Stop bothering her! You know she doesn't like it.

KHULSOOM: *(Amazed and exasperated—throws arms in the air)* Hanh, of course like always, father and daughter team up against the evil, tyrant mother.

HAKIM: How about you two women team up and give an old man some food, eh? And Fatima, wake up that brother of yours. *Kya poora dhin soyga?*[25] Comes from college, sleeps all day, awake all night…

FATIMA: Ghafur, get up! Ghafur! We're all waiting for you! Don't make me come up there—I swear if I come up there—

(As FATIMA goes to the back of the stage and yells upstairs, the lights fade.)

---

[25] "Is he going to sleep all day?"

SCENE IV

THE CASE OF THE
THREATENING NAIL CUTTERS

TIME: *A couple of minutes later.*

SETTING: *As before.*

AT RISE: *The family members in the family room. GHAFUR enters from the foot of the stairs.*

GHAFUR: (*Sigh*) And a silence permeates the air. What did I miss?

SAL: (*Annoyed, looks up*) That is *the gayest* thing I've heard all day.

FATIMA: (*Slightly bitter*) You didn't miss a thing. Just the same nonsense.

KHULSOOM: (*Suddenly changing her mood and tone*) Oh, Ghafur. Come here. (*Gives him a kiss*) Salu, don't call him a gay! Thoba!

HAKIM: (*Chuckles*) The elephant finally wakes up. *Kya poora dhin sonay walay thay?*[26]

---

[26] "Were you going to sleep all day?"

34

GHAFUR: Just couldn't sleep last night—jet lag. Some work I had to—usual stuff—

FATIMA: PlayStation 3, Xbox 360, Wii.

(*SAL curiously observes GHAFUR up close. He is looking at his beard and his skullcap. He playfully teases him and punches him a bit, in an older-brother fashion.*)

SAL: What is this? (*SAL looks at GHAFUR's kufi.*) And what is this disgusting mess? (*SAL looks at the beard on GHAFUR's chin.*) This filth. You put Velcro on your face?

KHULSOOM: Today is someone's birthday!

(*GHAFUR starts reddening, becomes a little embarrassed.*)

SALMAN: Whose?

KHULSOOM: Your son's twenty-first birthday—

FATIMA: Ami, it was supposed to be a surprise.

KHULSOOM: Oh, surprise, shmurprise. I couldn't keep it in. So, you thought we forgot?

SALMAN: (*Eyebrow cocked, surprised, then smiles*) Kya? Ghafur is twenty-one now? Hanh? (*Looks at KHULSOOM for the approving nod*) Mashallah, kya baat hay. Our little big man now. Come here, Beta.

(*GHAFUR goes over to his father, who hugs him with his right arm and kisses his cheek. GHAFUR wipes the kiss off.*)

GHAFUR: Thank you, thank you. Okay, okay. No big deal, just another day. More important things to think about.

HAKIM: Come here, Ghafur badsha.

(*GHAFUR puts his head down toward his grandfather's chest. HAKIM brings GHAFUR close to whisper something in his ear.*)

HAKIM: No longer the boy who used to jump on my back during my prayers. Now a full-grown, handsome man. Mashallah. You can carry me now on your back—

GHAFUR: (*Jerks back a little, shakes head modestly*) No, no, I can't—

HAKIM: (*Stern but playful, slapping his grandson's cheek*) Of course you can't! I'm not going to make you carry me! Allah has still given me strength in these legs to walk, inshallah, till the day I keel over and die. (*HAKIM puts his left hand around GHAFUR's neck—then gives out an agonizing yelp.*)

HAKIM: Ah!

GHAFUR: (*Helps him*) Kya? What?

(*Everyone takes a cautionary pause and looks.*)

HAKIM: (*Still grimacing*) Ah, nothing... nothing.

SALMAN: Is it the injury?

HAKIM: Yeah—heh heh. The bloody thing still lingers after all these years.

GHAFUR: Are you okay?

HAKIM: Yeah—nothing. Just fine. (*Sits down*) I told you, Beta—I still have the strength—like an ox. No falling down for me—not yet.

SAL: One of these days, you're gonna have to tell us how that happened.

HAKIM: (*Very serious all of a sudden*) I told you already. Just an accident… during the army days. Nothing…. nothing worth discussing. (*Relaxes*) Anyway, look, Ghafur, your ami spent the entire morning making your favorite for you—go, go give her respect.

GHAFUR: (*Brings both palms together*) Mmm, lamb biryani. Amazing. (*Goes to his mother*) But dangerous. Ami, why do you torture me? What are you trying to do, get me fat? I've already gained ten pounds. (*Shakes his stomach*) I'm obese.

KHULSOOM: Hanh, well—good. Least I can do—you don't accept any presents. Becoming some extremist. It's bad enough you have to eat outside food or cans of soup all the time in college—you come back to me looking like some Somalian. Allah knows how long it's been since you've eaten home food…

GHAFUR: I swear I eat your food all the time.

KHULSOOM: Jhoot—lies!

SALMAN: You freeze him enough food to feed his entire apartment building, plus all the jinns and genies that live in that city as well!

GHAFUR: Yeah, listen to Abu. No need to worry. This semester's supply didn't run out till two days ago—when I was on the plane. The airline thought the "Moslem Meal" meant the "no taste, no fish, no seafood, nonedible-substances meal." Once I saw that steamed lettuce next to that slice of tomato, I busted out Ami's khorma and curry.

(*KHULSOOM smiles.*)

SAL: Such an FOB, I swear—

37

FATIMA: Wow, they allow you to bring food on the planes? They didn't examine it under some antiterrorist lens?

GHAFUR: No, you can bring food, they give you that, at least—no sharp objects, though. They took away my nail cutter—

SALMAN: The one I got you?

GHAFUR: Yeah—the fancy one. Sorry, Abu.

SALMAN: Bastards! Idiots—totally incompetent. (*Muttering*) Well, did they give it back to you?

GHAFUR: (*His face drops.*) Uh—I was in a rush. Uh—no offense, Abu. An *awesome* nail cutter, but it was either the three-hundred-dollar flight or...

SALMAN: Hmph, or the nail cutter. (*Looks as if he's thinking seriously*) Hmmn, I would have done the same.

KHULSOOM: Why did you have to pack a stupid nail cutter, uloo? Idiot! Great, make them lock you up next time! You read—you should know better. The FBI probably has a file on you now!

FATIMA: "Probably" is being naïve. They *definitely* do.

GHAFUR: I don't know—

FATIMA: You're lucky they didn't just strip-search you, hose you down, and do some Superman scan of your internal organs while they were at it.

SAL: They did! And all they found was two-day-old Pakistani food sitting in Ghafur's stomach, slowly transforming him into Super FOB. (*Throws his hands in the air and fake bhangra-dances*)

HAKIM: Now all the elderly Muslims—even the Indian Hindus and Sikhs—are seen as terrorists. *La Hawla wa la Qhuwata!*[27] (*Sighs*) Inshallah, Allah will show us better days—

GHAFUR: I haven't told you guys the best part—

KHULSOOM: There's more?

GHAFUR: If life were only that easy, Ami. So—I pass the whole sandal-bomb, pat-down, scanning place and I'm heading to my gate. I sit there. I'm waiting, you know—the usual—everything's cool. The lady comes on the PA system—

PA LADY: (*Voice-over*) Attention all passengers, Flight 570 is boarding at Gate 18D. Economy passengers, seats ten through thirty, please board now.

(*As PA LADY's voice is heard, the lights dim on the family area. GHAFUR walks downstage, FATIMA and SAL handing him his bag and book, and arrives alone, downstage center, in a special light. GHAFUR addresses the audience now; the rest of the stage is dark.*)

GHAFUR: I pick up my bags, and I get in line. This article I'd read came to mind all of a sudden. It talked about how a crew of flight attendants refused to fly with a Punjabi Sikh man onboard. Even though the man was an affluent, tax-paying college professor—of English, no less—with American citizenship, he was kindly asked to leave so as not to *endanger and disturb the psychological and mental comfort of the airline passengers.*

---

[27] "There is no power or strength except with Allah." A common expression uttered when faced with calamity or disgust.

FEMALE FLIGHT ATTENDANT: (*Voice-over*) Um, sir. We'd appreciate kindly if you would please kindly leave the aircraft—quietly… and *quickly*. Thank you… *kindly*.

GHAFUR: Perhaps they think all people who wear turbans are terrorists? Perhaps they didn't like the way he looked? Maybe he smelled funny? Maybe he made the mistake of smiling at the attendant? Regardless, boom—he's off!

FLIGHT ATTENDANT: (*Voice-over*) Buh-bye!

GHAFUR: Which brings me back to myself, standing in line, wearing sandals, with a grizzly beard, with my prayer cap on, a *Sports Illustrated* in my back pocket and a new paperback of *Jihad and Terrorism* (*shows the audience the book*) under my left arm. The lady says—

FLIGHT ATTENDANT: (*Voice-over*) *May I see your boarding pass, sir?*

GHAFUR: She scans it. She looks at the screen. She looks at me—and the smile is now gone. She nods her head—a large Filipino man comes and takes me to the side.

SECURITY MAN: (*Voice-over*) Sorry, sir. Just a usual procedure. Can you please step aside for a moment?

GHAFUR: Um, have I done something? Is there anything wrong?

SECURITY MAN: (*Voice-over*; *nervous chuckle*) Heh-heh. No, no, just standard procedure is all.

GHAFUR: They spend five minutes doing a body search. They check my wallet, my keys, my belt, the contents of my bag, the magazine, my shoes, the keys again, and finally back to the belt. The other passengers stroll on by, witnessing the Muslim-mammal zoo exhibit. I'm sure it made them feel really safe, that I was being sanitized. Even safer, when I boarded the plane and walked down the aisle. Oddly enough—no one else was searched except a young black man and a middle-aged white guy. He probably had an Eastern European name.

(Lights go back up)

SALMAN: We'll sue the bastards!

GHAFUR: Please, relax. It wasn't that big of a deal.

FATIMA: What do you mean? Are you retarded? It's blatant racial profiling. They only nabbed you 'cause you had an Arab-sounding name—that's the only reason!

KHULSOOM: Didn't I tell you to shave your beard before you came? Who gave you the brilliant idea to keep a beard? And you wore the *topi*?[28] Oy, uloo! Why didn't you hold a sign saying, I'M AN EXTREMIST. ONE WAY TICKET TO ABU GHRAIB, PLEASE.

SAL: Relax, Ami. The government can't do anything to Ghafur. He's American, and a college student. They only deport those damn fundamentalist Arabs and illegal aliens that come into this country. Rightfully so, if you ask me.

FATIMA: *(Sharply)* I—God! You just—I'm not even going to start.

SAL: Relief!

GHAFUR: No, it's okay— you can't blame 'em—it's their job. I mean, it's America—we're scared of everything. Who knows, maybe I'd be the same way if I was Average Joe American.

---

[28] "skullcap"

KHULSOOM: My beta will be the healer of the world, hay na? The doctor who not only makes money and has status, but also gets prayers from the sick and, inshallah, heaven in the afterlife.

HAKIM: Ameen, Ameen.

GHAFUR: Perhaps there are better ways to heal the world than to become a doctor in this day and age.

SAL: Yeah, join a multinational corp. Voilà. I'm telling you—technology and globalization will unite, not destroy, the world. (*Makes triumphant operatic noises*) Ahhhh haaa aaahh ahh...

FATIMA: I don't know whether to laugh at your naïveté or your ignorance.

GHAFUR: Come on, Sis. Back off. I mean, Bhai has a point—usually people with food and homes don't go around blowing themselves up.

SAL: Except terrorist suicide bombers—

FATIMA: Or a people so brutally oppressed they have nothing left to lose—

GHAFUR: Except their lives, or maybe their humanity, I don't know—

SAL: Thank you, Noam Chomsky.

KHULSOOM: What? Are you going to college to learn politics or to learn doctoree, hunh?

SALMAN: Chup! Don't listen to your mother—it's good you keep up with all this. It's important. Inshallah, you can change all these policies *after* you've graduated from medical school.

HAKIM: Just don't chase the world, Beta. Muslims were never meant to limit themselves—gain knowledge and do righteous works for the sake of Allah while you still have your youth.

KHULSOOM: Ghafur, don't read too much of Rumi. I'm all for this changing the world and everything—and this goes for all you *pagals*[29] (*referring to FATIMA and SAL*). But first get the degree, get a job, *then* do whatever you want. Just get that degree first. I don't want my children becoming duffers.

SALMAN: Inshallah, it won't happen. All our children will become successful, well-known, respected members of their community. Our friends will envy them.

GHAFUR: I don't seek envy, I just...

SAL: (*Puts arm around him*) Stop with your aw-shucks Jimmy Stewart routine. (*Punches him*) Be a man. To be envied is divine—it's a good thing. Even an Islamic thing.

FATIMA: I highly doubt that.

SAL: Sure it is, according to normal Muslims, not fundos. Allah never said not to make bank, wear Armani, buy a Tag, marry a beautiful wife—at least not when I went to Sunday school.

FATIMA: You never went to Sunday school.

SAL: (*Quickly*) Two months—*more* than enough.

GHAFUR: There's more in this life than just—than a nice 401(k) plan, job stability, and medical degree. Those are all fine, but—

---

[29] "crazies"

KHULSOOM: But what? What's not to like, hunh? Sounds like a successful future, and you should be thankful you're not like those starving faqeers in Pakistan, or the homeless who beg for money.

(*GHAFUR, becoming increasingly annoyed, starts pacing. He puts his hands over his head, and then snaps.*)

GHAFUR: All right, great! Can we just eat food now? You've all been yelling at me to get up for the past two hours just to eat, right? Well, here I am—(*cools down, to appease the family members*) and plus I could smell it all the way upstairs. (*Sniffs*) Mmm, biryani.

HAKIM: No one listens to the old man—at least listen to the boy. Take out the food! I'm hungry and old. And you know how old boodhas get when we're hungry. (*HAKIM rubs his stomach.*)

KHULSOOM: Fatima—help take out the food.

(*FATIMA rolls her eyes. She helps KHULSOOM put food out on the table, going to and fro from the kitchen. Late lunch/early dinner is about to begin. HAKIM is already seated, waiting to eat. SAL, who has been sitting a little removed from the dining table, still looking at his phone, slowly comes to join them. GHAFUR is the last to arrive. He has been looking at the television. CNN, which was on at the beginning of the scene, is now heard again.*)

THE TELEVISION: (*Voice-over*) The president urged the nation today not to fear or doubt, even though the battle against extremism and evil will be long and painstaking, with unfortunate but inevitable sacrifices. According to the president, these sacrifices are necessary to ensure our freedom, and to help protect the liberties and values of *all* freedom-loving people against those dedicated to tyranny and hatred—

(*GHAFUR shuts off the TV and turns to join the family as the lights fade*)

SCENE V

JUST GIVE THEM
SOME LOLLIPOPS

TIME: *About thirty-five minutes later.*

AT RISE: *The family is now resting in the family room after eating a rather large meal. SALMAN is seated in his chair. HAKIM is sitting on the main couch, facing the audience. GHAFUR sits on the main couch next to HAKIM. SAL is separated from most of the family and seated in the kitchen at the table. Visible to the audience, FATIMA is seated with him, doing some work. KHULSOOM is in the kitchen as well. HAKIM leans back, rubs his belly.*

SALMAN: (*Looks at GHAFUR*) Like your birthday dinner—lunch?

(*GHAFUR is watching TV, so engrossed he doesn't turn his head to reply.*)

GHAFUR: Yeah, yeah, great. Alhamdulilah—it's just great—like always. She didn't have to, you know, I mean, just for a birthday—no big deal—

45

(SAL goes back to playing with his cell phone. He is watching stocks, reacting.)

SAL: Dammit! Man—I can't believe… this is why—I can't believe I didn't see two bulls drop. *(SAL looks at GHAFUR, who is staring at the TV.)* Yo! *(Snaps)* Television—MSNBC—money report—now!

GHAFUR: Yeah—just hold on. They have this special on—

SAL: Fascinating. Change.

GHAFUR: No, dude, I want to see this—just hold on.

SAL: Change it.

FATIMA: Just relax—so what? Some *rich* people lose money. Big deal.

SAL: *Some* money that is *earned* by *me* by working hard. You know—work? Labor? Place of employment—which I can't get to when you block the roads with your commies.

FATIMA: They're not communists.

SAL: Tell them to watch the ending of *Rocky IV*, all right? American Capitalist Rocky wins. Communist Soviet Ivan Drago loses. Ghafur *(in Russian accent)*, *I vill crush you* if you don't change the chan—

FATIMA: You know what? Yeah, turn it on. I want to see this. These stupid fools—*(looks at SAL)* running around tearing their hair bald just because some red numbers flashed the wrong way on the screen. I'll make the popcorn.

HAKIM: *(To SAL, trying to calm the situation in a gentle, elderly fashion)* Just let him watch. He rarely comes home. He'll change it in a sec—

SAL: He's been watching this crap for an hour!

GHAFUR: Five minutes. (*Beat*) Ten, tops. Okay, fifteen.

SALMAN: (*Exasperated, looks at GHAFUR*) Beta, just put it on for him, okay?

SAL: (*Sudden change, sharp*) Forget it. Never mind.

SALMAN: (*Caustic and little angry*) Fine. *Theek.*[30] Gave you a chance. Watch. Here, I'll turn up the volume—(*SALMAN takes the remote from GHAFUR's hand and raises the volume.*)

CNN HEADLINE NEWS: (*Voice-over*) The Soldiers of Peace, an Evangelical group with a loyal membership headed by Reverend Edwards, spiritual counselor to the president, say they are ready to send over two thousand, as they call themselves, "*lovers* of Christ" to help preach the gospel as soon as the army decides it is safe for American citizens and missionaries to reside in Iraq—

(*SALMAN dims the volume.*)

FATIMA: Soldiers of Peace—at least they're not subtle about it. And I thought this wasn't a crusade.

HAKIM: (*Visibly disgusted*) Just like the British—typical colonizers, imperialists, just like the *ferengi*[31] Europeans. Come in—rape, loot, destroy, turn brother against brother and countryman against countryman just for dawlat and power. Man never changes.

GHAFUR: (*Digesting all the conversations*) At least these Christians—well, the good ones, the well-intentioned ones—not this Edwards guy— at least they're trying to teach—

---

[30] "Okay."
[31] "foreign" (derogatory)

SALMAN: Preach!

GHAFUR: Or *teach* people about their Christianity.

FATIMA: Yeah, right! How Christian is it to bomb innocent civilians? And then conveniently convert the devil-inspired heathens—that's us, by the way.

SALMAN: Muslims—we deserve this. Useless. All of them—Saudis—whoring their oil in exchange for their Amreekan allowance. Turkey—the "Sick Man of Europe"—trying to be more European than Europe. The Iranian Americans—HA!—*finally* protesting *something*! They're only out there because they think all the Macy's sold out of blue contact lenses. These Yemeni Arabs, so pious with their liquor stores at every street corner. And Wahabbis—*kumbakhts*![32] Spreading their Wahabbism with their millions to the Taliban, and Pakistan, and—

FATIMA: Politicians' pockets.

HAKIM: Politicians... *soowar ki awlad*![33] Seen all types of them in my life—Amreekans, Hindus, Muslims, Christians—all progeny of pigs. Will sell their mother for a vote or a profit. Men, we never learn. We keep putting flags on this earth and actually think we own or control something—forgetting that Allah is the *Malik al Mulk*, the King of His Kingdom.

SAL: (*Shakes his head*) Is this why I'm missing my show? (*Wipes some sweat off his head.*)

---

[32] "bastards!"
[33] "progeny of pigs"

FATIMA: What's your opinion, huh? You have one?

SAL: My opinion?

FATIMA: Yeah.

SAL: My opinion. In the end, it's economics. Simple economics. Always has been, always will be.

FATIMA: And how about morality and ethics?

SAL: For. Sale. Morality? Please. I'd rather have these "reborn" Christians than those militant Muslims, all right? One group can hold hands, do some koombayas, and cry like babies over a campfire and the other can prepare for *jihad*!

FATIMA: Typical. You'd sell them out, wouldn't you?

SAL: (*Sharply*) Yeah, and so would you.

GHAFUR: (*Quickly interjects*) That's what I'm saying. These extremists using those millions to teach their perverted version of Islam. The Taliban thinking it's Halal and Islamic to beat and lock up women. Thinking they're doing God's work. Americans, and these Christians here, thinking each and every Muslim is a Jew-hater, about to go berserker-rage and blow himself and everyone else up. No one knows anything. And look at this media—that's the same garbage they get day in, day out. And no Muslim does anything— we just sit and complain. Why don't we go out and tell them how it really is? You could do it. (*Looks at his dad*)

SALMAN: Yeah, right. And you can earn the daily bread.

GHAFUR: You can! Call over all these neighbors—do a potluck. We've lived here fifteen years and I don't even know most of their names. Go to those churches and do some interfaith dialogue.

FATIMA: Yeah, and get fifty St. James Bibles and What Would Jesus Do stickers.

GHAFUR: Well, at least you'll have tried.

SALMAN: (*Smiles proudly—taps GHAFUR on the back*) Alhamdulilah, good. It's good. We should do this. All these are excellent ideas. See? This is why he should be the president of the Muslim College Students. Hay na? (*Commandingly*) Next year, run for it! Implement all your ideas. At least one of my sons takes some interest in the religion. *Dekhe, Abu?*[34] (*Looks to his father*) I always said he was the smartest one, from the beginning.

HAKIM: No, you always said that he was the most talented one. And Fatima the most passionate one. And *Salahuddin* (*stresses the name*) the smartest one.

(*KHULSOOM enters now*)

KHULSOOM: Kya, what is all this? *Phir se,*[35] politics. I leave you all for five minutes and politics, politics, politics. Enough! Can't you all talk of something else? Hanh, Ghafur—especially you? When did you become one of them? Fatima, have you been poisoning his mind with your nonsense?

FATIMA: Great, just great. Blame me always. The middle child always becomes the voodoo child. I have more important business to take

[34] "See, Father?"
[35] "Again"

care of than to be guidance counselor to Ghafur.

SALMAN: Inshallah, my son will become the best of doctors—everyone will see and take notice.

KHULSOOM: God willing! Ameen.

GHAFUR: Is that so?

SALMAN: Is that so? (*Chuckles*) Of course, nothing less can be expected from you.

KHULSOOM: He's just humble, that's all. It's good to be humble, but not so much that you become a doormat.

HAKIM: *Nahee, nahee.*[36] Don't listen, it's good—be humble. Prophet Muhammad, salalaho alayhi wa salam, was always humble, so there's no reason a doctor can't be.

KHULSOOM: As long as he's a good one, not a third-rate penniless one stationed in the ghettos somewhere, Allah forbid.

GHAFUR: I've decided I want to be a teacher.

(*A sudden silence—a pause from the entire family. ALL heads turn toward GHAFUR.*)

HAKIM: Kya, Beta?

KHULSOOM: What? What!

SALMAN: Beta—did you say, heh heh, you want to become a teacher? Hah!

---

[36] "No, no."

FATIMA: I think that's what he said.

SALMAN: (*Still chuckling*) Well, good. I also one day want to teach, *after* I retire from the company. It's noble work, teaching people—you get rewards for it in this world and the next. You have good ideas! You'll be a good teacher, when you're an old man… after you've done medicine.

GHAFUR: (*Calmly*) I'm not doing medicine.

SAL: Oh, this will be awesome! (*Shocked like everyone else in the family, SAL says this with a wry smile, leaning forward with anticipation. KHULSOOM's mouth remains open. SALMAN is slowly becoming angry.*)

SALMAN: You're… You're what now?

GHAFUR: I said I'm not studying medicine—

SALMAN: No, I heard you, but I heard you incorrectly. You're what now?

HAKIM: (*Trying to calm him*) Beta, relax, just listen to him, he—

SALMAN: No, no, I *am* listening to him, but I'm not hearing him properly, because probably I'm becoming old and my ears are filled with too much hair. I just thought I was paying all that money, working like a dog for the past three years for chemistry books and biology lab reports and—

SAL: (*Sharply*) You have plenty of money—

SALMAN: (*Sharply*) What would you know about it—just some loafer!

KHULSOOM: How could you decide this? When? Why wouldn't you *tell* us about your decision? Why are you ruining your future? All our plans we had for you—

GHAFUR: All *your* plans for *my* future.

SALMAN: (*Snaps*) Your future *is* our future! It was decided long ago! We made a decision—that's why I pay that goddamn money for that goddamn private school!

GHAFUR: (*Takes a breath, very calm—looks toward his parents*) And I'm grateful for it. I never said otherwise. But—you made *my* decision for my future. *My* future. My decision, without ever asking *me*. No disrespect to you or Ami—

KHULSOOM: Hanh! No disrespect to us! Of course not! Good, Ghafur. What are we? Just two old people who gave birth to you, took care of you, cleaned you, cry and pray for you every night? Who are we? Nothing—

SALMAN: Just some worthless old pieces of shit! That he can do away with now that he's an adult—thinks he's an adult because up and away he goes to college. Starts thinking for himself and (*mockingly*) *his* future—telling me what he's going to do. Well, as long as I pay the bills—you are becoming a damn doctor. And a good one at that! No, no, not a good one, the best! The absolute best! (*eyes drift slightly, as if he's pensive*) So they can never cut you down, or humiliate you, or take away your hard-earned rewards. No son of mine (*looks at SAL*)—sons of mine—is going to become some third-rate, penniless professor teaching little kids grammar and sentence-vocabulary structure and whatnot.

GHAFUR: I don't plan on teaching children.

KHULSOOM: (*Melodramatic*) What will the community say? Our nose is cut. I brag and brag about you gaining admission to the top university, scholarships, Shabnam's beta, Riffat's daughter, Saima's two kids all becoming doctors—all of them envious and jealous of you. Now what? They will be rich in ten years, and you'll be getting apples from two-year-olds.

FATIMA: Relax! God, just listen to him!

SAL: (*Shakes head like a seasoned veteran and smiles*) Who has time to listen when everybody loves hearing their own voice in this house?

HAKIM: (*Soothingly*) Beta, just—*araam se.*[37]

(*SALMAN has processed nothing. His anger and frustration is rising.*)

SALMAN: That's right! You shouldn't plan on teaching anything, because you're not doing it! That's it! I will not discuss it further.

GHAFUR: Inshallah, I'll get my doctorate.

KHULSOOM: Hanh, good. (*Sighs in relief*) Then go teach.

SAL: (*Smiling*) He means doctorate as in professorship, Ami. As in PhD: Pakistani Has Doctoree.

KHULSOOM: (*Nervous*) Is that what you mean, Beta? Nahee.

(*GHAFUR nods his head in affirmation.*)

GHAFUR: Inshallah, in history with emphasis on the Middle East, Islam, and Arabic. It would be ideal to be tenured at a prominent university like Harvard, Columbia, or Berkeley, but if I can't be, then Allah knows best. I'd even teach elementary or high school.

---

[37] "be calm and relaxed."

FATIMA: (*Taking GHAFUR's side*) Yeah, they need good teachers, especially at the inner-city schools by our college. There are a lot of Muslim kids there who don't know anything—

KHULSOOM: High school? High school!?!

GHAFUR: Why not? Like Fatima said—at least I'll get the opportunity to make people unlearn all the misinformation they've been force-fed their whole lives about Muslims, Islam, Arabs, and the Middle East. And inshallah, Abu and you will get the blessings of my work.

SALMAN: Don't bring religion into this. Using it to cover up your lying and deceit! Hunh? What—no, no, humiliating your parents, that's part of the Qu'ran and Sunnah, right? Now he's teaching me about Islam—like I'm an idiot! *I* don't know anything. Lying to me and using my money! Making *a* jackass out of me all this time!

HAKIM: He's just trying to—

KHULSOOM: Teach Islam? Kya, you want to become some mawlvi, some scholar and give fatwas? (*Looks to sky*) We have enough blessings, Allah thera shukar. You can bless us by becoming a surgeon. You like kids? Become a pediatrician; teach them Islam as you give them their lollipops!

SAL: (*Looks to GHAFUR, very coolly*) The sad part is—she's serious.

KHULSOOM: *Ya Allah, teri madad*![38] What has overtaken our Ghafur? All these hippies and liberal friends at your college, brainwashing you, making you lose your focus. Fatima and her friends… (*Looks at daughter*) This is your fault!

---

[38] "Oh God, help us!"

HAKIM: Beti, you're speaking through anger. You're not being rational!

FATIMA: (*Explodes on mother*) Yeah, yes—there you go, judge! Case closed. My fault. *I'm* guilty. It was me all along. I confess. Me and my covert—(*trying to find words, looks at SAL, finally finds the word*) *ninjas* infiltrating Ghafur's mind with propaganda. 'Cause I have nothing better to do than to waste my time—because *of course*, according to you, I do *nothing* but waste my time, because all my activities are supposedly *useless* to backward women like you!

KHULSOOM: (*As if looking to a jury, pleading her case*) See? See? This is what I was telling you about. This... these are my *awlad*.[39] Can't believe I gave birth to them. Instead of listening to their parents and taking care of them, they want them to grieve and die as fast as possible, so they can have their freedom—and marry whomever they want, or go become some faqhirs... doctors, teachers in the ghetto!

FATIMA: Oh, great, great, it's okay for you to yell and scream at me, but God forbid I lose my temper. Then I'm like the devil who wants you to die? Right, makes rational sense. Great argument.

SAL: (*Looking at the chaos like a spectator watching a circus*) This *is* more exciting than the stock exchange!

SALMAN: (*After hearing all this, turns to his father*) Please put some aql and sense into him, like you did to me? Please, my permission—slap him. (*Anger rising*) Beat some sense into him if you want!

(*SALMAN goes into the kitchen, shuffles hurriedly through some drawers, and brings back a spatula. He waves it toward HAKIM.*)

---

[39] "children"

SALMAN: Here—take this. (*Anger rising*) Go ahead! Beat it out of him. He's obviously had it easy. Didn't have to work hard, earn his keep, sweat his way to the top like his parents. The morons who don't know anything! Please, Aba, please!

(*SALMAN thrusts the spatula into HAKIM's hands. HAKIM looks flushed and embarrassed—saddened. He raises both his hands, as if he were either praying or hiding his face. Perhaps he is doing both. He shakes his head lamentably and just sighs.*)

HAKIM: *Ya Allah, ya Rahman, hamaree madad kar. Koy tho sunay?*[40] *Koy tho sunay?*

FATIMA: Abu, relax!

HAKIM: Just be calm, be calm. Listen to the boy. This isn't the end of the world!

SALMAN: He's destroying his life before it can even have a beginning!

GHAFUR: At least I'll be responsible for my own downfall—

(*SALMAN suddenly and loudly slaps GHAFUR. SAL explodes off his chair and runs to defend his brother. Everyone gets involved in stopping the fight.*)

SALMAN: So, you're going to fight your father again?!

SAL: If I have to!

KHULSOOM: Abey, *hato!*[41] Choro! Hato! He's your father! Salahuddin!

(*SAL comes to his senses, puts his head down, storms off.*)

---

[40] "O, Allah. O, Merciful, help us. Won't anyone listen?"
[41] "stop!"

HAKIM: Salman! *Kya pagal ho gay ho?* Have you gone mad? Acting like some madman. What did I say? Let him speak! Go—go to your room! You, too—go with him!

(HAKIM motions for KHULSOOM to take SALMAN upstairs. SALMAN has already cooled down considerably. The anger has left his face. He is tired and perplexed by his actions. KHULSOOM takes him by the arm and starts leading him out toward their bedroom. SALMAN stops a moment and looks toward GHAFUR.)

SALMAN: Ghafur—are you—I didn't mean to. I—just don't... don't talk of this. Not today. I don't want to hear it—not today. We'll talk about it later. Later. Not—now. (*Suddenly becomes more passionate*) It's just this heat! This goddamn heat! Makes a man crazy—(*looks at GHAFUR again*) I—Fatima, make—make some chai for me.

(SALMAN looks to KHULSOOM. FATIMA just stares at him. Then she exits. SALMAN leaves with KHULSOOM to the upstairs bedroom. HAKIM motions for GHAFUR to join him on the sofa.)

HAKIM: Your father can be pigheaded and stubborn. But he loves you, you know that. He didn't mean to—

GHAFUR: (*Still calm, reeling over slap, hand on cheek*) I know. I know he didn't mean it. I know, it's okay. I don't mind. Ami, too. I didn't expect it. Actually, I expected much worse. (*Chuckles*) Got off kinda easy, no?

HAKIM: Your father, he... planned everything, Beta. He had such dreams for you. The first doctor of the family. The family in Pakistan, everyone here, they all expect so much out of you.

GHAFUR: (*Very calm and cool*) I realize that. But I won't allow other people to create my expectations. And I won't be a slave to others' expectations of what I should or need to be.

HAKIM: Well—it is your life, Beta. That's true. But there is respect for your parents, as well. You—all of you—can't let go of our traditions. Respect! Respect for our way of life! If you lose it, your parents, me, we... we've all failed you and our ancestors. Your father—he... shouldn't have slapped you. You know him, his anger, like bread—rises for a moment then suddenly disappears. He'll apologize—

GHAFUR: It's all right, just—forget it. Forget it.

HAKIM: Just rest for a bit. Don't worry, we'll figure this all out. Inshallah, everything will be golden for you, Beta. It always has. All of my grandchildren—all unique pieces from the same shining star. (*Looks to GHAFUR*) Allah is the best of planners, remember that, Ghafur. Look to Him, bachay, and He will guide you. Inshallah, He will guide us all. (*Pauses, looks down as if lost in thought*) And perhaps forgive us, as well. (*Gains awareness*) We all... just need some rest.

(*HAKIM exits stage left with GHAFUR, toward his room, as the lights fade.*)

THE REVENGE OF THE I.M.B.E.S.

TIME: *A little while later.*

SETTING: *We see a boy's bedroom decorated like a high-school kid's room. There is a bed. The bed is messy and has luggage on it. There are some clothes on the floor. There are some toys in a toy basket. Pictures of Homer Simpson and Joe Montana are on the walls, next to a painting by Van Gogh—one of his sunflowers. There is also a green banner that reads* LA ILAHA ILL ALLAH, MUHAMMAD-AN-RASUL ALLAH.[42]

AT RISE: *SAL picks up a partially broken Starscream Transformers toy. He plays with it, trying to transform it back to its original robot shape. He is amused by this toy: a relic of his childhood. But he grows frustrated by his inability to change it back to what it was.*

---

[42] "There is no deity but God, and Muhammad is the Messenger of God."

SAL: (*Playing with the toy, talking to himself. Spotlight on him. Background in relative darkness.*) I'm playing with this nasty Transformers toy in my old bedroom when I could be at work taking care of some business. Abu has proven to me he's officially gone insane, Ghafur wants to be Mary Frickin' Poppins, and the whole family has come out in full circus-freak glory. What a day—what a day! Can't wait to see what happens next.

(*GHAFUR is now lit. He is lying down on the bed—pondering, with eyes to the sky—oblivious to the world. SAL notices him now; he comes up close to GHAFUR's face, inhales, and then blows hot air in his ear. GHAFUR suddenly jerks back. SAL does it again. GHAFUR punches SAL's arm playfully. SAL starts dancing his fingers in front of GHAFUR's eyes, making weird noises.*)

SAL: *Weeooo, weeeooo.*

GHAFUR: Stop it—cut it out, Bhai.

SAL: (*Pauses, cocks a smile*) I know you, Gay-fur. You can fool the rest of 'em, but not me. The Ghafur I grew up with thinks of the two steps he's gonna take before he even takes his first one.

GHAFUR: Whatever.

SAL: This whole teaching business. Knowing you, I bet you decided earlier. Last year. Summer of high school? Aren't I right? Huh?

GHAFUR: Yeah, you know me all right! *Everyone* knows me, supposedly. *Especially* Ami and Abu. But (*abrupt change of tone*) it's okay. I don't blame them. It's not their fault. I should apologize for—

SAL: No, damn it! It's not all right! Stop *apologizing* for me and everyone else in this goddamn house. You don't have to be Sir Lancelot, the shining… frickin' Boy Scout all the time. You've got this—(SAL *taps* GHAFUR's *head*) and you know it. But you don't have *these*. (SAL *grabs his private regions.*) *Never* apologize for those two. Immigrants to the new motherland, have the Amreekan baby, and the Amreekan dream. Make all the stupid mistakes you want. Don't worry about fixing it, just *lay* the blame on the culture and the environment or the kaafirs or the youth. Messed up with the firstborn.

GHAFUR: You're not messed up—

SAL: (*In a fake, immigrant, authoritarian "adult voice"*) Whoops—realized we weren't too pious in the oat-sowing days, sorry, number one, let's make it up with number two. Whoops—didn't teach number one Urdu; afraid he won't fit in.

GHAFUR: Fit in a little too well, didn't you?

SAL: Mess up with the first one—no problem. Polish it up with number two. Purrrfect in draft three.

GHAFUR: Didn't you hear what went down? I'm giving lollipops to black kids in the ghetto. Perfect? Is that what you really think?

SAL: I don't think it. I know it. It's true.

GHAFUR: Seriously now, lay down the crack pipe, Bhai.

SAL: Right after you, Father and Mother's pet. Abu (*shakes his head in disgust or sadness, unable to decide on either*)—that guy—what a piece of work. Practically disowns me.

GHAFUR: He doesn't disown you.

SAL: What do you know? You've been gone. How would you know what's happening here? Mr. Golden Child—Golden retriever, more like it. (*Makes a panting, puppy-eyed, domesticated-dog face while looking at GHAFUR*) I get pissed on left and right for twenty-seven years, each side of the face, and I say screw it—I don't have time for this bullshit, and I leave—and what? Does he ever once ask me to come back? (*Voice is cracked, starts choking up, albeit briefly*) Even once?

GHAFUR: So you'd come back if he'd ask?

SAL: (*Suddenly regains his composure and flippant attitude*) Hell no—that's not the point.

GHAFUR: What *is* the point? What are you trying to say? Just say it. Go ahead. Everyone's had their shot. I've been waiting for yours.

SAL: What I'm saying is I *am* tired—(*SAL points to GHAFUR*) of you and your beard. And this kufi or whatever. (*In mocking voice*) Becoming a professor or whatever. Listen, you want to teach? I don't give a shit. Teach. Teach Ping-Pong to Cheech and Chong. Just do it because *you* want to. Don't do it for anyone else. And you know what? You're eventually going to do *noth*-ing.

GHAFUR: (*Shows a brilliant, small flash of anger. But mumbles the following under his breath in a controlled yet slightly sharp fashion*) Yeah—I'll follow in your footsteps.

SAL: (*Just as quick as GHAFUR*) And then you might *finally* get some chicks.

GHAFUR: (*He must have his quick jab*) Inflatable dolls don't count.

SAL: I'm giving you reality—and I'm not even charging you my flat fee. All you're gonna do is *think of doing* something noble. There will be no jihad, no selfless poverty, no feeding the homeless, no noble sacrifice—*nothing*! If you have to remember one thing, Ghafur, remember this: you have to be a *bull* in this world. A bull among the cattle. (*Mimes this with hands and fingers as he speaks*) You take your aim and you *run*; no stopping; no looking back; no regrets about leaving the little people behind. Survival of the fittest *and* the smartest. And know that in the end, if it's between the bull and the cattle, the bull will not hesitate. It will ram any obstacle out of its path. The bulls of the world are the people who succeed, Ghafur. Me! Everyone else is just cattle. (*Points to GHAFUR's heart*) This, bro, this… is gonna be your downfall. I'm just lookin' out for you, is all.

(*There is silence in the room. FATIMA shakes her head. She has entered during the monologue and now stands, listening, near the doorway. GHAFUR ponders what he's heard.*)

FATIMA: (*Sarcastically*) Just the kind of advice I was hoping you'd give him.

SAL: Listen, I'll be damned if I'm gonna wipe someone's ass and tell him it smells like peaches. (*Turns to GHAFUR*) Ask yourself this question, oh wise sage; it's an oldie but goodie. (*Turns around and dramatically says*) Do I dare disturb the universe? Figure that one out and you might have an idea where you're going.

FATIMA: I'm sure that's exactly how T. S. Eliot meant it.

SAL: T. S. Eliot is dead.

(*Phone rings*)

SAL: But I'll—(*SAL says his next word with a sarcastic, melodramatic flair, obviously making fun of FATIMA's vocabulary.) hasten* my chance to meet him with my good friend Marlboro here and this—business call. *Excusez moi. (SAL steps outside the bedroom.)*

FATIMA: *(To herself)* Great, memorizes one line from "Prufrock" and thinks he's some intellectual. Psycho-freak. Just wish Abu and he would finally bury the hatchet.

GHAFUR: *(Shrugs)* In whose back? But like he said, what do I know... I don't know anything.

FATIMA: He didn't say you don't know anything.

GHAFUR: Close enough, right?

FATIMA: *(Tries changing the subject by abruptly becoming melodramatic)* Like you all of a sudden becoming some professor? Hello! *(Pauses, abrupt break)* I mean—okay, it's great, I support you—I'm just saying—

GHAFUR: You're *just* saying, Bhai's *just* saying, Ami, Abu, Daada are all *just saying*. Only one not saying anything is me. But it's only *my* life, right? So, *mubarak*, congratulations—now it's your turn, Judge Judy. Step up and educate me. You're *just saying* don't become a teacher. Because, after all, you're *just saying* what's the rank of "educator" on the desi monetary hierarchy?

FATIMA: *(Smiles—backs off, understands and empathizes with her brother's increasing frustration)* Guessing probably somewhere in the lower part of the social food chain?

GHAFUR: Yeah, preceded by janitorial maintenance, followed by the job where you pick up dead animals off the highway, and finally "the art-iste."

FATIMA: Unless of course the art-iste happens to be a Bollywood megastar.

GHAFUR: Naturally.

FATIMA: Naturally.

GHAFUR: What if I create a new profession: the International Muslim Bollywood Educator Superstar. I.M.B.E.S. Immbbsse. Professor by day, dashing, FOB heartthrob by night. I'll drink my chai in slow motion, rip off my clearance-sale Calvin Klein, and whisper sweet nothings to my bee-u-ti-ful heroine.

FATIMA: I'm sure Ami and Abu will be proud of having an I.M.B.E.S. in the family. You'll get paternal approval the day I bring home a Black Prince. And we both know that won't be happening soon.

GHAFUR: (*Roles reverse. GHAFUR is now the soothing psychologist. FATIMA is lying on the "couch," metaphorically.*) People can change, Fatima. Ami and Abu can change. They'll come around, you'll see. Eventually. (*Pause. Says the next word with strength, hope—and doubt*) Inshallah.

FATIMA: (*Her tone becomes somber and sad—this is a side of her we haven't seen before, almost as if we're seeing a soldier remove her armor.*) People don't change, Ghafur. No one changes. In their head they think they've changed. In my head, I think I changed—evolved into a better Muslima, a stronger woman, more liberated, more fearless, ready to fight and take on the world—but it's all pointless delusions in the head. You just take temporary vacations from yourself, time to time.

But you always come back home. (*Pause*) Everyone—always, in the end, comes back home. Sometimes people just don't want to learn. Or unlearn. Their perspective—lifestyle, whatever you want to call it... It's their only reality—(*voice starts to gain some passion, but it's subdued*) even if it is narrow and ignorant and racist and an endless pile of denials and lies upon lies. (*Calms down, resigned*) For them—for us, for *me*—it only matters if it works... as long as it's safe and reliable.

GHAFUR: So I take it I'm not getting you a wedding present?

FATIMA: Oh, really perceptive there.

GHAFUR: Say what you will, I'm sticking to my original prediction about you two. It's gonna happen—

FATIMA: You actually thought they'd let me bring in a convert? Their only daughter marrying a convert, an *American* convert—

GHAFUR: Don't forget—who's bee-lack.

FATIMA: They'd rather I married a Hindu, as long as he's relatively brown.

GHAFUR: Well, don't give up.

FATIMA: There's no point. Ami probably saw me in a dream, roasting in some fire pit as lots of black people were dancing around me listening to rap music.

GHAFUR: With Aziz holding the torch.

FATIMA: Yeah, right. It's so sad. He's such a good person. And we did everything Halal. We haven't even done anything! And he's smart and kind and he's passionate. He doesn't drink, and even before converting he never messed with girls or drugs or any of that. And he knows Arabic, like, *fluently*—totally awesome recitation and accent. You'd think he was from Syria or something.

GHAFUR: Well, have you told Aziz yet?

FATIMA: No. He'd just get angry and say it's the same old cultural Scarlet Letter he's had to deal with the past seven years.

GHAFUR: You should tell him.

FATIMA: I know—maybe. Maybe. We'll see.

GHAFUR: (*Suddenly excited, like a student finding a solution to his problem*) The veil is about to be lifted, Fatima, I can feel it. Once it is lifted, people will finally see and experience the truth!

FATIMA: (*In her questioning, cynical tone*) The truth?

GHAFUR: The mighty Muslim Abbasids wiped out like trivial insects by the Mongolian hordes. All of Christian Europe devastated, crippled at every level by the Dark Ages, warfare, and the Black Plague. The Jews rounded up—killed, harassed, oppressed. But they survived, and Islam, Judaism, Christianity all returned... stronger, more vibrant. They never left. America, Americans, the world... paralyzed by fear, hatred, doubt. Perhaps it's a purge. All this is just a purge, you know? A purification. Allah preparing us for the universal Renaissance. Then they won't fear us. We won't fear them. I know it. It has to be—has to... Ami and Abu won't be afraid, either. None of us.

(*As FATIMA shakes her head and smiles, SAL abruptly comes in. He's a little steamed, and is talking to himself, although his voice is audible to his siblings.*)

SAL: Stupid horse teeth. Knew it. Never trust your eyes when looking at a woman in the dark. Always look at them in the light—and *without* makeup. Never trust their words—*especially* when they're wearing makeup—and a skirt. Dammit. Always same mistakes. Always stupid. (*Pauses before continuing*) Her loss. Nasty-ass, pasty-looking horse face. Too bad I don't speak horse code. (*Makes some braying Mr. Ed horse noises and dances around like he's mounted on a pony—then looks around*)

FATIMA: Thank you, Coach. I take it the *merger* isn't happening?

SAL: Oh yeah, yeah. The merger, right. Uh, no, it fell. I mean, I wasn't there—that's why. Not everyone can do it, you know. It takes talent. Finesse.

GHAFUR: And you have to be a bull, right?

(*SAL slaps GHAFUR's shoulder proudly and with passion, like a coach does a football player who's made a forty-five-yard touchdown catch.*)

SAL: Allahu Akbar! (*Looking at the sky*) He's learning! Can you believe it? He actually listens to me for once. You'll go far with that advice—trust me. Fatty, make me some chai!

(*SAL runs out of the room with FATIMA chasing him to battle, pillow in hand. They completely disappear into the darkness, until the remaining light is solely focused on GHAFUR, now standing. The rest of the stage is dark. GHAFUR appears to be looking directly at the audience, yet he is immersed in thought. After a five-second pause, he says:*)

GHAFUR: Do I dare disturb the universe? (*Takes some time; his face reveals the answer before his lips do.*) It's about time someone did.

SCENE II

KOLOR ME KASHMIR

TIME: *Sunset, maghrib time (the sunset prayer, fourth prayer of the day).*

SETTING: *Master bedroom.*

AT RISE: *We are shown a new setting, indicating a sitting area in the master bedroom. There is a laundry basket filled with dried clothes on the left side of the bed. Next to it, a pile of folded clothes. On each side of the bed, next to each pillow, there is a cabinet stand about two feet high. A mini-lamp sits on the right-side stand. A* Reader's Digest *and many other magazines are stacked on the bottom shelf. Atop the left-side stand are two picture frames, a dhikr bead, and a real-estate textbook. Islamic calligraphy is mounted throughout the room. There is a door to a bathroom.*

The bedroom has a window (not seen). There is a television set in the middle of the room (also not seen). As the lights come up, KHULSOOM is sewing at her "sewing station." Muhammad Rafi's "Barsaat ki Raat," a famous golden-age Indian song, plays in the background quietly as KHULSOOM hums sadly to herself, adrift in her own thoughts.

72

(*SALMAN enters from the bathroom. He has changed his clothes. He is wearing a simple white Hanes undershirt, Pakistani pajamas, and sandals. His face appears to have been washed, and there is still water on his sideburns—the face of a man who just dried himself with a towel. He is uppity and impatient. KHULSOOM doesn't notice his entrance. She is still humming. SALMAN picks up a shirt from beside her. He smirks at her, inspecting the shirt, disgruntled.*)

SALMAN: *Sathya naas.*[43] He ruined it. Everything—everything for me, like always—just falls apart.

KHULSOOM: (*Defensively*) He didn't ruin it. I fixed it. It's just like new. You're always being melodramatic. Over a shirt.

SALMAN: (*Quickly turns, addressing her sharply*) *Abey, pagli!*[44] Who cares about this shirt? I have hundreds like them! Collared, striped, unstriped, buttoned, not buttoned. (*Disgusted as he says this*) This is nothing. Just cloth. (*Pause—anger rising again*) A useless, cheap, good-for-nothing—(*SALMAN examines the back label*) Made in Bangladesh, I knew it! A second-class Pakistani made this! Makes sense! Worthless piece of cloth. (*Flustered with disgust, SALMAN eyes the clothes on the bed. He rummages through the clothes, picking up a shirt or two that isn't folded*) Look—this shirt, ruined! This is supposed to be dry-cleaned. I've told you more than a thousand times—

KHULSOOM: These are all cotton! I've told *you* a thousand times that it doesn't matter if you dry-clean them or not. You always take care of it yourself, and whenever I do it, you yell at me because it isn't perfectly the way you like it—

---

[43] "Ruined."
[44] "Crazy lady!"

SALMAN: That's right! The way I like it! Me! The *showhar*,[45] the man of this house, the husband whose right it is to demand some small things that bring him some peace! But my *badkhismatee*[46] is that I'm surrounded by—by villains, who—

KHULSOOM: (*Shocked and outraged, but not an angry outburst*) Villains?!? *Acha*?[47] Theek. So this is now a Bollywood movie, and you are the hero, and I, being the wife, the *ghulam*, the one who is the cause of all of life's problems, will have everyone's *nazla* and *zookam*[48] thrown on me?! (*KHULSOOM puts her fingers to her nose and mimics throwing snot from her nostrils.*) I'm the villain?!

SALMAN: Hanh, *ghulami*? Servitude? You don't even know the meaning of the word. To you, doing some simple house chores, performing some requests for your husband, has become *slavery*. Why don't you go write a book now? I'm sure it'll be a best seller. Put it in Barnes and Noble or on Amazon.com—*Ghulami: The Suffering of the Muslim Wife*. Or maybe this one—*My Husband, the Pakistani Slave Driver*.

KHULSOOM: I'm your wife, but I'm nobody's ghulam. I'm not the deaf, mute village girl who hops on one foot waiting to serve her master—

SALMAN: I'm your master? You don't even give me half the respect a person does the chokidaar, or the janitor or the bathroom attendant! A woman who doesn't even bother to cook biryani with chicken for her husband, just one damn plate of chicken biryani! Can't even bother to dry-clean two shirts! No wonder *your* kids turned out this way—

---

[45] "husband"
[46] "bad destiny"
[47] "Okay?"
[48] Literally, this means "cold and flu," but it is used to signify grief and complaints.

74

KHULSOOM: Oh, so they're mine now, not yours? Just because you're angry with them, all of a sudden I had a miraculous conception— (*Pause*) *three* (*shows three fingers, saying this sarcastically*) miraculous births, mashallah mashallah.

SALMAN: You and your sarcasm. And this is what you've taught your kids. This is why they've turned out the way they have. Look at Salahuddin. Such disrespect—and now Ghafur? I thought at least one of my sons inherited my Hyderabadi manners, but even he acts like a junglee[49] Punjabi now! (*SALMAN starts mimicking Punjabi bhangra dancers, carelessly throwing his hands in the air, hopping about a bit and making noises.*)

KHULSOOM: This Punjabi is the one who gave birth to them, taught them their prayers, washed their bottoms, took them to school, and went to every PTA meeting! While you, the Hyderabadi, like all Hyderabadis, talk the talk—and ruin the language while you're at it. Did you sacrifice your career and studies to look after Salahuddin and Fatima? Who was here while you went and got your masters and traveled abroad?! Who was the one who left her family behind in Pakistan?

SALMAN: You want me to give you an award for doing all that? You're supposed to! That's what mothers do! You want your reward, inshallah, you'll get it in heaven! Although with these kids—the way they've turned out—we're destined for jahannam and hellfire! And my travels abroad? Like I was gallivanting in Nepal or Bermuda with my seventy virgin houris! Not working eighteen-hour days like a dog just trying to provide something for my family and some

---

[49] "Uncouth"

75

luxury for you, so your precious *naak* (*Points to his nose*) wouldn't be cut in the community!

KHULSOOM: I never wanted any of this! (*She looks around and points to random commodities.*)

SALMAN: Hanh, *now* she doesn't want any of this. You don't want the fine house in the suburbs, the jewelry and the nice saris, the perfect Persian and Indian living-room set.

KHULSOOM: I've put up with enough of your belittling through the years, Allah is my *Gavah*,[50] but I won't let you impose your vanities and insecurities on me!

SALMAN: Vanities? Vah—vah, what English!

KHULSOOM: I can tell you in English, Urdu, Punjabi, and languages only wives and mothers know! *You* were the one who always wanted the *mansion*, and the BMW, and the big-screen TV. The *dunya*[51]—all these—these *things*. Shiny, gold, marble things to be seen by people. To be seen as the *big* man, with the respect and wealth.

SALMAN: Hanh, but that doesn't stop you from driving the BMW? Or mentioning to Ghafur, "Oh, what will the community members think?" And you've bought these sharp designer jackets and shoes you wear for your clients. You're the one trying to impress people!

KHULSOOM: You don't even know your wife in all these years. You don't even understand that I'm not working for the money. I couldn't care less for it.

---

[50] "Witness"
[51] "world"

SALMAN: That's what they all say when they have it.

KHULSOOM: Money doesn't comfort me! You don't even understand; you're working most of the time. Fatima off to law school, Ghafur only comes on holidays now, and Salahuddin—just your abu and me in this house—

SALMAN: Blaming me now for the kids staying away from you?

KHULSOOM: They stay away from *you!* Except Fatima—your favorite. She sees me as a backward masi who only knows how to cook and clean. And my boys, you already drove one away! And now after hitting Ghafur, I've probably lost both of them.

SALMAN: You want me to be sorry for hitting him? His whole life I've hit him two, three times, each time barely a slap! Here, your son Ghafur is a liar! Deceives me, deceives us! Salahuddin—arrogant, angry, and rebellious from the beginning—

KHULSOOM: He reminds me of you.

SALMAN: Take a look at Fatima sometime, and *then* look in the mirror, Mrs. Freud. Ghafur lied to us—me! One slap is nothing at all. He's deserving of more than that, let me tell you. I—I lost my temper, but who wouldn't have? Any other family, he'd probably have been kicked out of the house, like your friends Shabnam and Riffat—

KHULSOOM: I thought you didn't care what others think of you!

SALMAN: Your kind ruins everything when they open their mouths. (*Pause*) I should've married a village girl. There were dozens of girls lined up for me, all begging for my *rishta*.[51] At least with one of those

---

[51] "engagement"

I would've gotten a decent meal, a dry-cleaned shirt, and some silence.

KHULSOOM: (*Insulted and angry*) If you want some silence, then try shutting up for once! And you're not the only who had rishtas lined up, *sumjay?*[52] Mine weren't village boys, either—(*beat*) they were doctors! But it seems you didn't want a wife, you just wanted a slave. Who is the one who prays *every day* that your projects are successful? Thanks Allah—every night—for your good job, and hopes your company finally sees how brilliant and deserving you are of that promotion—even if it means you staying away for a year or two! I'm sure you would've found dozens of girls like that—but you wouldn't have someone like me. Your partner, and your best friend!

(*Upon hearing this, SALMAN looks away from KHULSOOM and walks toward the window. His gaze extends past the view. He remains silent, but it is obvious he is pensive. After witnessing this, KHULSOOM drops her aggressive and confrontational stance. She is worried, all of a sudden, and curious, but she knows the answer to her next question.*)

KHULSOOM: They didn't give you the position, did they?

(*SALMAN, still looking out the window, shakes his head no.*)

KHULSOOM: I knew it.

(*SALMAN quickly turns around, suddenly animated.*)

SALMAN: How? Who? Did Abdullah's wife tell you? I bet it was his mother. Couldn't wait to rub it in, I'm sure—*kameenay.*[53]

KHULSOOM: (*Calm and assuaging*) I've been married to you almost thirty

---

[52] "understand?"
[53] "terrible people"

years. I know your face. You were upset when you walked through the door this morning.

SALMAN: Upset? Too much to be upset about in this world. Disappointed, yes—who wouldn't be? A man works, faithfully, competently, not a single blemish on his entire record, night and day, like a dog. As they say in America, give a dog a bone, or throw one—at least once in a while, right? This brown, foreign, Muslim dog—a Muslim camel. Not even a camel jockey. Hunter, the executive of my division, loves his camel-jockey and A-rab jokes. It's been thirteen years and he still thinks I'm from India. "India, Pakistan, Afghanistan, what's the difference?" he always says. My name was too hard for him to pronounce, so he asked me, or rather told me, (*SALMAN does a hick accent*) "I'ma gonna call you Sal from now on. You don't mind, now? It's hard for Americans to pronounce these A-rab names. You understand me, Sally?" And from that day on I was "Sally" to him, and "Sal" to Brian the CFO, and "the Sal Man from Pak-is-tan" to all the interns and assistants. Theek, I said. Theek. At least they have some of the name right. "Everyone takes a beating," Abu always said that. He told me, right before I left for Amreeka: "Remember, Beta, those streets in Amreeka aren't paved with gold, they're paved with blood. As a foreigner, you're going to take a beating, you'll always take a beating. But inshallah, when you make your gold, don't wipe your blood off the street. Keep it there, to show all of them that you've *earned* it." And all I have after all these years is a bloody nose and a bloody shirt.

KHULSOOM: They gave it to Abdullah? Abdullah—the graduate student? Didn't he join just—

SALMAN: Eight months ago. Twenty-eight years old. I helped him get a job. Heard there was a position, and I, trying to be a good Muslim, helping my younger brother in Islam, recommended him.

KHULSOOM: I'm sure he wasn't even grateful.

SALMAN: Nahee, nahee. He was. For six months it was Uncle Salman this, Uncle Salman that, thank you so much, I'm forever in your debt. Kumbakht![55] Haramzada! Jhoota!

KHULSOOM: You should tell him to step down and give it to you!

SALMAN: This twenty-eight-year-old kid. This kid—Salahuddin's age. Wears a daarhi, his beard down to here—(*points to chest*) looks like Osama bin Laden's younger brother! This fraud—this is the one they chose for the new contract! No one was more qualified or experienced than I in that entire department, and who did they give it to? Abdullah! Not because he's smarter or more talented or more hardworking, all the qualities that matter. Hunter told me:

HUNTER: (*Voice-over*) Sally, my boy, we love you here, you know that. But we've decided to give this job to one of your boys, *Ab-doolah.* I knew you'd be happy—heck, you can barely contain your surprise or excitement, I understand. We're sending Ab-doolah because here's a young A-rab man who is absolutely serious about his Middle Eastern Ar-a-bic roots, and dedicated to his religion and culture, and it's *exactly* that image we need to drive home to our foreign investors and current business partners—that we, as Americans, respect their exotic culture and A-rab-esque heritage, and to prove it, we're gonna send 'em one of their own—*Ab-doolah!* That "authentic" image we're gonna sell them needs a certain kind of representation that

---

[55] "Idiot!"

only Ab-doolah, God bless 'im, has in spades. But don't worry, Sally, you'll be working for Ab-doolah here in the States—giving him all the assistance and help I know you're capable of. God bless ya.

KHULSOOM: (*Flustered*) This is not fair. This isn't right. This is exactly what you said—racism! Discrimination! We can talk to the ACLU or CAIR and tell them you were passed over for—

SALMAN: For a Muslim? A Muslim passed over for a Muslim. For a Muslim who acts and plays the part.

KHULSOOM: You act and *are* the part! They all know this. You should have gone into Hunter's office and *demanded* he give you the job, or else—

SALMAN: Or else, what? Or else I'd quit?

KHULSOOM: Yes, quit! No one needs to be a *chamcha*, a spoon for these racist gorays.

SALMAN: You're a chamcha in this world no matter where you go. Just another utensil to be used and thrown away.

KHULSOOM: You just can't let them *do* this to you! To us!

SALMAN: I'm tired, Khulsoom. And I'm old. They knew I wouldn't quit. I could never fit the part. Lord Ab-doolah will be a millionaire in less than five years. And I'll continue to occupy my position, faithfully, as the sepoy who never dared to rebel.

KHULSOOM: I've never seen you quit in my life! If you think I'm going to sit here, as your wife, and watch you deflate like a—a *naan*—then you don't know your wife and you don't know yourself, either! Leave that job! We don't need them! Alhamdulilah, I make enough money

SAL: I learned it from you.

SALMAN: A pity you didn't learn anything else.

SAL: Learned the rest on my own.

SALMAN: Hanh, while you were paying for your baby clothes, and diapers, and teaching yourself to do math and drive also, right?

SAL: Yeah—well—

(HAKIM cuts them off.)

HAKIM: Bahu, chai! Where is this chai? Your mother, your wife, I tell her not to make this new-age hippie-vippie, modern chai.

KHULSOOM: (*With some sarcasm*) Chai has been ready for some time. I was only waiting for the hookum and order.

HAKIM: Theek, *nikaalo*.[66] For everyone.

(The tension is slightly relieved. SALMAN increases the volume of the TV, and all can hear it as KHULSOOM brings out the chai on a tray.)

FEMALE COMMENTATOR: (*Voice-over*) This war will end only when these monsters and terrorists and Al-ka-eeda and fundamentalist regimes renounce their hatred and extremism and learn to love and embrace democracy and freedom and American values, such as tolerance and separation of church and state and, God willing, good hygiene, ha!

MALE COMMENTATOR: (*Voice-over*) Ann, how do you expect them to love us when we're invading their countries and bombing their homes?

---

[66] "Take it out."

FEMALE COMMENTATOR: (*Voice-over*) That's the problem! They don't understand. They just don't get it. We're *not* invading them. Hello, stupids! We're *liberating* you!

FATIMA: (*Turns off the TV*) Okay... I just... I just don't even know what to say. Is she serious? Do commentators on TV actually hear themselves when they talk? They must be insane. That's it. I won't watch the news anymore.

KHULSOOM: That's what you said last week.

FATIMA: Well, last week I didn't see this lady.

SALMAN: This woman has the best-selling book in the country right now. Her entire audience is paranoid men and women who think I'm going to bomb their house and convert their children.

GHAFUR: (*Not responding to his father, but merely giving his opinion*) Her audience is the same as all the right-wingers. Just like the other guy, his audience is only the left-wingers. There's no balance.

KHULSOOM: Left, right, middle, conservative, liberal. What happened to normal?

FATIMA: It got hijacked.

HAKIM: *Chai achee hai,*[67] Bahu. I'm glad you didn't put grass and herbs in it.

KHULSOOM: I never put that in my chai.

FATIMA: It's called *ginseng* and *rose hips* and *peppermint*.

---

[67] "The chai is good"

SAL: I don't need this—

(*As SAL storms off, he inadvertently knocks into his grandfather, causing him to spill his hot chai. HAKIM yelps in pain and drops his cup on the floor. The chai splashes everywhere, some of it on HAKIM's arms, legs, and shirt. It is very hot. The family members jump up and run toward him.*)

HAKIM: (*Yelling in agony*) Ah!

SALMAN: Abu—

FATIMA: Are you okay?

KHULSOOM: Oof, go, Fatima, hurry, get the sponge and some paper towels!

GHAFUR: Are you hurt?

SAL: (*Apologetic, complete change of character*) I'm sorry, I'm sorry! I— I didn't see it. I didn't mean to… I was just…

(*SAL bends down. He takes the sponge from his mother and starts to clean up, trying to help his grandfather.*)

SALMAN: Leave it. You've done enough! Are you happy?

GHAFUR: He didn't do it on purpose.

SAL: Listen, I—it was a mistake—

KHULSOOM: Here, choro, I'll clean it!

SAL: (*Very stubbornly, sounding a lot like his father*) No, let me. Just— leave it!

(*KHULSOOM backs off, a little startled. SAL simmers down. He shakes his head and drops the sponge. As he starts to leave, he notices the teacup on the ground, and bows to pick it up. HAKIM has removed himself from the couch, and stands a few feet apart from his family. His eyes become red and almost teary.)*

HAKIM: Did I ever tell you what I used to do in India? (*His eyes are glazed.*)

KHULSOOM: (*Hesitant, quickly tries to cut off HAKIM*) You—you're *hurt*. You don't have to tell us stories now. You can tell us *later*. Fatima, clean up the—

GHAFUR: No, I want to hear what he has to say—

FATIMA: Daada, you don't have to tell us anything if you don't want to, you're hurt...

SALMAN: Tell them. Tell them everything. They want to grow up.

(*HAKIM, positioned center stage and talking directly to the audience, begins his story. He is physically present but immersed in his nostalgia.*)

HAKIM: I remember it so clearly... It was August 16, 1947—two days after the official partition. India and Pakistan received their independence from the British. In our village, we were all happy that at least the British, *beymaan*[69] kameenay, would no longer use desi land for their profit. But it never takes long for the devil to do his work. As is the way of men, some calling themselves Sikh, others calling themselves Hindu, and others saying they were Muslims, none of them could bear to live together. Each claimed the land as their own. Some fought for religion, or for politics. Others fought out of petty rivalry, or mere jealousy. Sikh killed Muslim. Muslim

[69] "dishonorable"

killed Hindu. Hindu killed Muslim. I kill your brother, you kill my family. I burn your store, you burn my house.

GHAFUR: You saw this?

HAKIM: At least my village was spared this at first, and I just did duaa so that I could teach, and live a good life. A peaceful life. But this world is not a world for peace, only torment and hardship. That day, a mob came to our village. A mob of Hindus with hate in their eyes. They were looking for my neighbor Amir, saying that he was a thief and had looted one of their stores, and his Muslim friends were defending him.

Khayr, I didn't know if he had stolen something or not, but it didn't sound like it was worth much trouble, hay na? And plus, I'd defend my friend—even a thief—especially from a Hindu mob. Matter of principle. You never let your friend fall!

So I lied and said I didn't know where he was. They went from house to house. Umair, another Muslim, was hiding him. In front of my eyes, all our eyes, they told him to come out, said they only wanted to talk to him. As soon as he came out, they took a knife and thrust it into his chest. I couldn't move. I did nothing. Nobody did anything.

I had never seen a man die before—and my friend Amir, he was stupid and used to chase girls and shoot off his stupid mouth—but not deserving to die. And they killed him, and I did nothing! I was so afraid I couldn't move. We were all witnesses, and testified to the police. We waited one day, two days, they did nothing. We went again, and they told us to mind our own business if we knew what was good for us. One week later, Umair was found hanging from a tree. They cut open his stomach and let his guts hang out. And I did nothing. And they kept killing and killing. One more

Muslim and then another. And since the police chief was involved, of course his men did nothing.

FATIMA: Did *you* do anything?

KHULSOOM: *Ub, buss.*[70] Enough of the story. We know it already.

HAKIM: (*Oblivious, in his own zone*) So I thought, What if this was me? Who would protect my wife? Corrupt cops, judges bought out by bribes, just as happy to see the Muslims killed as the ones who killed them. There were a few Muslims who took justice into their own hands—men who made a pact to punish those who killed our people and got away with it. One slain Muslim brother would equal ten grieving Hindu widows! So I joined these men. And I learned how easy it is for a man to lose his soul.

The first life you take is the hardest—that one you can never forget. After the first, the rest became routine. I hunted each and every one of them. I grabbed one while he slept next to his wife. His baby girl was there, too. It did not matter to me. All I knew was that he was the one who killed Amir with a knife, so I knifed *him*—right in the chest, as his wife watched, yelling for mercy. She was talking to deaf men. Then there were the two who killed Umair and hung his body like some worthless, sacrificed goat. We killed them and hung their bodies from the same trees, *high up*—to show all of them, anyone who could see, that killing our people would not be tolerated!

The others we caught, blindfolded, and lined up in one row. I took off their blindfolds. Many were in tears, speaking in any tongue they knew, praying to their Gods, my God, begging me

---

[70] "Now, stop."

to spare their life. I took my gun and kept shooting until all my rage and anger were emptied into their dead bodies. We left them to rot by the river. If I had a thousand bullets it would not have been enough.

GHAFUR: Oh, my God. How could you do that? Why didn't anyone tell us this before?

HAKIM: They put a price on your daada's head. They killed two of my companions. My Hindu friend Amit, of all people, warned me that they were coming for me. So I took all the money I had and I gave it to your daadi and had her leave for Karachi—not knowing if I would ever see her again. Saleem and I, the only ones remaining, were wanted men.

After weeks of running, we were near the Punjab border. We were so close, but Saleem was starving, so we stopped in a bazaar to have some food. (*Sigh*) Qismat. Destiny. Allah is the best of planners. As we drank chai I thought of your daadi, and her masala chai. (*Inhales, as if remembering its taste*) Mmm... Allah had put such flavor in that woman's hand. And I wondered if she was alive and if she had made it to Karachi, and Allah knows why, but my hand shook and I spilled the chai all over my lap and dropped the cup on the floor. Saleem, who always looked up to me and followed my every order, went to grab it.

I had never been shot before, so it was a new experience. I felt an intense, burning sting. Almost as if a jinn had come and grabbed me from inside. *Ajeeb*, I thought, why is there blood coming from my chest? And then I saw Saleem. The bullet had gone through his neck and into my shoulder. A bullet meant for me killed my best friend instead. This was just one of four bullets that other men eventually took for me. Their suffering ended and mine began.

(Everyone is stunned.)

GHAFUR: How did you survive?

HAKIM: Only Allah knows. That time I took my knife, said, "Ya Allah," and ran toward them, blindly waving and slashing the air. I thought I was dead, and I made my peace with Allah, knowing I would one day have to answer for the blood I'd spilled, and that other men would have to do the same. But—as was Allah's will—I survived. I just ran until I was lost in the crowd. And I kept running until I made it to Pakistan. In a way, I have been running ever since.

This scar is forever a part of me. It reminds me of the violence, the hatred, the death, the suffering that I both experienced and was responsible for. What do you or anyone on TV know of this? By talking about it, you think, *they* think, you can understand what it means to kill someone? Or to see your friends you've known your whole life killed, just because one calls himself a Muslim and another a Hindu? Some say don't use violence, use peace. What happens when violence comes after you, and you just want to teach poetry and study law? What happens when you kill, and instead of earning your death, your friends are killed instead? Is that just? Is that fair? No one can know or understand until they have to face that reality. And I pray none of you ever do.

This scar—it is *my* punishment. The physical pain is nothing. I would give *anything*, my entire life twice over, just for the memories to go away. Just to *forget* the screams. But I cannot. And, whether you like or not, it is a part of me, so it is a part of you.

(All silent for a moment.)

FATIMA: I... I can't believe you never told us this! Pathetic! Here I am respecting Daada all these years, because he was some glorified army officer in Pakistan—

GHAFUR: But of course that's probably all a lie as well.

KHULSOOM: Your daada *is* a respected officer in Pakistan. And each family, from that time, each family has some history.

GHAFUR: But you didn't have to *lie*. I mean—all those men killed. You could have forgiven them, or made them pay blood money—

FATIMA: Or taken them to court. Or used the justice system. Bribed them, just like the others paid bribes. You could have used diplomacy or talked to them...

SALMAN: Weren't you listening to him, Miss Barrister?

(HAKIM smiling.)

FATIMA: It's not funny. You have blood on your hands! *We* have blood on our hands! And you're smiling!?

HAKIM: Diplomacy is only a word used in politics. Reality is what we and others had to face.

GHAFUR: You could have easily walked away—

SAL: As they killed his friends?

FATIMA: So you would have killed them as well? Great. Now I understand this family completely. This is why we're so messed up. We have the curse of God knows how many innocent men killed by Daada on our entire lives.

HAKIM: None of us was innocent. Each of us went mad in our own way.

GHAFUR: You can at least atone for it, right? I mean, you must feel guilty, right?

FATIMA: Why even tell us in the first place? I mean—I didn't *ask* to know this. I don't want to know this.

HAKIM: What you would like to know or not know doesn't matter. What matters is that you know the truth, and that you now confront it and make some peace with your history.

FATIMA: This is *not* my history. My history is just being an American Muslim who is in law school, and the worst thing I've ever done is to be arrested for protesting and standing up for what I believe in. And to try to marry a respectable man—even if he is black!

KHULSOOM: Fatima!

FATIMA: (*Not paying attention, still after her grandfather like a litigator*) After all these years, when you look back, would you have done *anything* differently? I mean, after all that death and chaos?

HAKIM: (*Thinking silently for a moment*) I don't know. I just did what I felt was right at the time. Not a day goes by that I don't remember my actions or the men, all of them, who were killed. The Muslims, Hindus, Sikhs, and Christians. But I, I—cannot change the past.

FATIMA: And that makes it okay?

SALMAN: Fatima, *buss! Chup ho jow! Thum ko kya maloom?*[71] You don't know how it was in those days. How could you? (*Looking at FATIMA and GHAFUR*) How many men and women and

---

[71] "Enough! Be quiet! What do you know?"

children died just trying to cross the border? Houses burned down, businesses destroyed, women raped—what would you have done? Or you? Or any of us?

HAKIM: She'll make a good lawyer—one that I could never be.

GHAFUR: I would never have killed anyone. That's for sure.

HAKIM: Man can't decide that, Ghafur. Life sometimes decides for you.

GHAFUR: No, man is always supposed to control himself and his actions! Just because—just because everyone else is going nuts, doesn't mean I have to—or will!

SAL: You don't understand anything.

FATIMA: Yeah, and you do?

SAL: No, I don't know anything. A person can never really know until he faces that situation. You have to trust yourself at that moment and do whatever it takes. Even if that means making the wrong decision. As long as you take a stand and act honestly.

(HAKIM *looks at SAL. SAL looks back, as if he has understood something.*)

FATIMA: I just—I just don't get it.

HAKIM: (*Trying to change the topic*) Don't get anything. You've just had chai. Araam karo, relax a little. Everyone just relax. It's hot and I'm tired of talking and hearing you all talk and talk. And I'm old, and now I'm hungry. Isn't there supposed to be cake on birthdays? What type of ami doesn't get her son a cake on his birthday?

KHULSOOM: (*Mood lightens up*) Well, this ami has always gotten a cake for her child's birthday.

(FATIMA is shaking her head.)

GHAFUR: Yeah, but that doesn't have anything to do with it. I mean, I still don't get how you can—

SALMAN: It's not chocolate, right?

KHULSOOM: Don't start with me.

SALMAN: Hmph, chocolate. Couldn't get vanilla.

KHULSOOM: It's Ghafur and Salahuddin's favorite.

SAL: *(Grudgingly)* Is it ice-cream cake?

KHULSOOM: Does your mother know you?

SAL: Well—I'll stay—just for a bit. For cake. *(Looks at his father)*

SALMAN: At least for cake. We can all stay for cake. What is a birthday without cake?

GHAFUR: Yeah, and how about presents?

FATIMA: I knew it—the Sufi thing was just an act.

GHAFUR: I'm just saying—

(KHULSOOM has the cake ready to go. She dims the lights and brings it to the family room. She starts singing and they all join in, everyone off-key and out of sync. She sets the cake down in front of GHAFUR, and, after putting one candle in the middle, lights it.)

ALL: Happy birthday to you... Oh, happy birthday to you... Happy birthday, dear *Ghafur*... Happy birthday to you...

SAL: Make a wish.

(GHAFUR closes his eyes, makes a wish, and blows out the candle as the lights fade to black.)

END

BIOGRAPHICAL NOTES

WAJAHAT ALI (*playwright*) is a Muslim American of Pakistani descent. *The Domestic Crusaders* is his first full-length play. Born and raised in the city of Fremont, in the San Francisco Bay Area's Silicon Valley, he has been writing, producing, and directing plays, films, and comedy sketches since he was a child, enlisting his friends to serve as actors and crew. In the fall of 2001, during his undergraduate studies at UC Berkeley, he began writing *The Domestic Crusaders* in order to fill a twenty-page short-story requirement due for a writing class taught by Ishmael Reed. With Reed's encouragement, he transformed the piece into a play. It premiered in 2005, at the Thrust Stage of the Berkeley Repertory Theatre. In 2009, *The Domestic Crusaders* premiered off-Broadway in New York at the Nuyorican Poets Café; by the end of its five-week run, it had broken the café's box-office records.

Ali's essays and interviews on politics, the media, popular culture, and religion have appeared in the *Washington Post*, the *Guardian*, *Salon*, *Slate*, *McSweeney's*, the *Huffington Post*, *CNN.com*, the *Wall Street Journal*,

CounterPunch, and *Chowk*. He blogs at *goatmilkblog.com*, and is the associate editor of *Altmuslim.com* and a contributing editor to *Illume* magazine.

In 2008, Wajahat Ali was honored as an "An Influential Muslim American Artist" by the U.S. State Department; in 2009, he was recognized by the Muslim Public Affairs Council as an Emerging Muslim American Artist, and selected as a Young American Muslim leader by the Center For American Progress. He is also a practicing attorney in the San Francisco Bay Area.

CARLA BLANK (*director, dramaturge*) has served as artistic director of the Domestic Crusader Project since 2003, mounting staged readings and performances of the play. She recently collaborated with the director and designer Robert Wilson to create *Kool—Dancing in my Mind*, a performance portrait inspired by the Japanese choreographer Suzushi Hanayagi. *Kool* premiered at New York City's Guggenheim Museum in April 2009, and a film related to the production aired on French television in May 2010.

Blank made her professional debut as a choreographer/dancer in 1963, as a participant in a Judson Dance Theater Workshop performance in New York City. Her two-volume anthology of performing-arts techniques and styles, *Live OnStage!*, coauthored with Jody Roberts, is widely referenced in school districts throughout the U.S. and Canada. She is the author and editor of *Rediscovering America: The Making of Multicultural America, 1900–2000*, and with Ishmael Reed, she edited the anthology *Pow Wow: Charting the Fault Lines in the American Experience—Short Fiction from Then to Now*. Her current projects include a study of North American women who became architects in the nineteenth century.

ISHMAEL REED (*producer*), the author of twenty-six published books and six plays, is also a lyricist, publisher, editor of numerous anthologies and magazines, television producer, radio and television commentator, teacher and lecturer, and blogger for the *San Francisco Chronicle*. His most recent publications include *Barack Obama and the Jim Crow Media: or The Return of the Nigger Breakers* and *Ishmael Reed, The Plays*; two new books—*Juice*, a novel, and *Bigger Than Boxing*, a nonfiction work on Muhammad Ali—are forthcoming.

The founder of PEN Oakland and the Before Columbus Foundation, Reed has championed the work of other writers as the editor and publisher of small presses and journals including the *Yardbird Reader*, *Y'Bird*, and *Quilt*. His current online magazine, *Konch*, and his current imprint, Ishmael Reed Publishing Company, can be found at *ishmaelreedpub.com*.

Two of Reed's books have been nominated for National Book Awards; a book of poetry, *Conjure*, was nominated for a Pulitzer Prize. He has received writing fellowships from the Guggenheim Foundation and the National Endowment for the Arts, and New York State Council on the Arts fellowships for publishing and video production. In 1995, he received the Langston Hughes Medal, awarded by the City College of New York; in 1998, a John D. and Catherine T. MacArthur Foundation Fellowship award; in 1999, a Fred Cody Award from the Bay Area Book Reviewers Association. Harold Bloom designated Reed's novel *Mumbo Jumbo* one of the five hundred most important books of the Western canon.

Ishmael Reed was born in Chattanooga, Tennessee, and grew up in the working-class neighborhoods of Buffalo, New York. For over thirty years, he taught creative-writing courses in the English Department at the University of California, Berkeley, retiring as Professor Emeritus in January 2005. He currently lives in Oakland, California.

THE DOMESTIC CRUSADERS
A PLAY BY WAJAHAT ALI
DIRECTION & DRAMATURGY BY CARLA BLANK

2005 CAST
Thrust Stage, Berkeley Repertory Theatre
July 15–16, 2005
San Jose State University Theater
September 10–11, 2005

KHULSOOM	VIDHU SINGH (Principal)
	NIDHI SINGH (Alternate)
FATIMA	SADIYA SHAIKH
SALAHUDDIN	KASHIF NAQVI
HAKIM	SAQIB MAUSOOF
SALMAN	SHAHAB RIAZI
GHAFUR	ATIF NAQVI

PRODUCER: Ishmael Reed
COPRODUCERS (SJSU production): Mitch Berman, Scott Sublett
PRODUCTION MANAGER, LIGHTING DESIGNER,
AND STAGE MANAGER (BRT and SJSU productions): Linda Young
DESIGN CONSULTANT: Sameena Ali
CAST PHOTO: Kashif Naqvi

THE DOMESTIC CRUSADERS
A PLAY BY WAJAHAT ALI
DIRECTION & DRAMATURGY BY CARLA BLANK

2009 CAST
Nuyorican Poets Café, New York
September 11–October 11, 2009

KHULSOOM.............................. NIDHI SINGH (Principal)
                                     DEEPTI GUPTA (Alternate)
FATIMA....................................MONISHA SHIVA (Principal)
                                     KHUSHBOO SHAH (Alternate)
SALAHUDDIN ....KAMRAN KHAN (Principal)
                                     PARAS CHAUDHARI (Alternate)
HAKIM ....ABBAS ZAIDI (Principal)
                                     SWARAJ SEHAJPAL (Alternate)
SALMAN ....IMRAN JAVAID (Principal)
                                     ATIF QURESHI (Alternate)
GHAFUR ....ADEEL AHMED (Principal)
                                     ALI N. KHAN (Alternate)

PRODUCERS: Rome Neal, Ishmael Reed
PRODUCTION MANAGER: Imran Sheikh
STAGE MANAGER: T. Pope Jackson
RESIDENT ARTIST: Rusty Zimmerman
SET DESIGNER: Jason Sturm
DESIGN CONSULTANTS: Sameena Ali, Farah A. Ansari
LIGHTING DESIGNER: Rome Neal
CAST PHOTO: Adi Talwar, courtesy of Ford Morrison Studio